Now...
Faith
Is...

How to Create the Life *God*
Desires for You to Live by Faith
and by Works (Action)

Fray White

World Inspirations International, Inc.
www.wii-inc.com

Printed in the United States of America
First Edition: September 2015
10 9 8 7 6 5 4 3 2 1 Library of Congress Cataloging-in-Publication

Data White, Fray Now Faith Is:
How to Create the Life God Desires for You to Live by Faith and by Works (Action) / Fray White −2nd ed ISBN 978-0-615-42512-2
1. Leadership— Religious Aspects—Christian.
2. Leadership—Biblical Teaching.

Dedication

I dedicate this book to my children: Olivia, Paigie and Fray Jr., for always loving me and my family who believed in me. More importantly, I thank God who has blessed me to have such a foundation of supportive friends to draw from when I needed them most. I could hardly begin to name them all. Thank you all so much! However, I will name a few.

My darling mother, Katherine Loretta White, who always says to me, "But seek Ye first the Kingdom of God and His righteousness and all these things will be added to you." Thank you mother! And my sister, Sheffrie White Butler, my (Best Friend) Vacation Bible Study buddy, who forever says to me, "Close your mouth!"

I give my sincere gratitude to Elizabeth Littlejohn and Pearline Anderson, the 'Big Sisters' God has given me, thank you! Lastly, I would be re-missed not to mention my Angel Investors who believed in me with their finances long before I finished my writing. Darletta Strothers and William and Karima Cameron. Finally, my dear friend Dr. Chandra Render for birthing the idea of me being a writer, by saying, "If you write a Book about Faith sir, you better be prepared to live it!" Thank you for that Truth!!

The Faith of a Son

Fray Jr.: "Dad, can you send me $100.00 dollars?"

"Fray, its 9:00 p.m. on Friday night, I can't get it to you tonight!"

"Dad, if you don't got it in a hundred, you got it in fifties."

"Dad, if you don't got it in fifties; I know you got it in twenties"

"Dad, if you don't got it in twenties; you got it in tens"

"Dad, if you don't got it in tens, you got it in fives."

"Dad, but I know you got it!"

Dad: "Fray, your money is at Walmart" (MoneyGram).

By 9:00 a.m. Saturday morning, Fray had his $100.00. His faith was so strong...` It moved me to fulfill his desire. I did not have any money at that time, but found a way to get him what he had faith for. Fray did not relegate me to a specific way. He just believed! I believe this is how God operates when we don't box Him in. He says: "And without faith it is impossible to please Him" **(Hebrews 11: 6)**.

Fray White Jr. (9 years old)

Contents

Preface

In all of history there is probably no better social climate to present an argument for reliance on faith. Less difficult times and circumstances tend to lead us to believe that we can conquer the world all on our own. In other words, we begin to believe in our own "ultra-self-efficiency." On the other hand, challenging times speak to the contrary and force us to pursue alliance with an "Enabler."

In the year 2000, Wolfgang Petersen produced a movie which held many movie viewers captive and on the edge of their seats as a likeable fishing crew embarked upon a fishing vessel called "The Andrea Gail." The craft took to sea in search of a plentiful fisherman's reward. Difficult economic times placed all of the crew in need of an immediate economic breakthrough. Little did they know this trip would be their final venture on the high seas.

They sailed into what meteorologists identified as the "Perfect Storm" – a unique set of weather conditions which converge in rare form from opposite directions. In the movie these factors all combined to create the storm of the century.

In August of 2012, after I had essentially completed the manuscript for this book, a storm (Hurricane Sandy) of epic proportions and even greater danger threatened the eastern seaboard of the United States. The timing was ironic and the results were disastrous to communities all along the coast. Popular seaside resort towns, famous boardwalks and amusement attractions were literally washed either to sea or forced inland to unlikely resting places.

This storm ravaged the area and added to another storm of sorts already brewing over the Nation for a number of years. However, the evidence of this lingering storm which is plaguing the entire country was circumstantial in nature. Unlike in Hurricane Sandy, there were no eroded beaches, tidal surges from the sea, uprooted trees, massive debris or cell towers devoid of power. This storm's beginning was almost subtle in origin, yet just as destructive. Financial indicators, political unrest, disintegration of the family (as God designed it) and global calamity had become a part of what had become the "new normal."

The storm continues and we find ourselves in the eye of the threatening system. In spite of the present **sociological** climate, we should not fear or resolve that we are sailing towards destruction like the crew on The Andrea Gail. Though analysts, media and political pundits paint a dismal portrait, we are not doomed like the crew in the movie to face destruction and despair. Instead, we are experiencing the real deal—an existence which is subject to and blessed by the will and grace of God.

In the movie, in spite of the crew's collective expertise navigating the sea, everything the fishermen tried began to fall apart. Unlike their journey, in our real life episode a way of escape is available and in place. It does not fail! When we are at the end of our ability to cope or produce desired results, God has provided a simple matter of faith which provides the courage to believe that there is an answer. Faith is the PERFECT answer for this PERFECT STORM! Its navigational component system will not lead us on a stormy sea without a way of escape. This perfect faith answer or response is closely connected to the basic mission assigned to the church of the living God!

Across Christian denominational lines it is generally agreed that the call to the church is to carry the powerful message of faith. Unlike the ill-fated ship in the movie, we're certainly aren't doomed to drown in individual circumstances—unless we choose to do so! Although various groups under the umbrella of Christendom fail to agree on many things, there is a consensus and commonality which embrace the promises of Christ; especially as it pertains to the message of hope and faith! It is my prayer that "Now... Faith Is..." will help to inspire you and provide encouragement, even in the midst of stormy seas, floods of doubt, turmoil and insecurity.

The Call to the Church (The Body of Christ)

Since a major charge given to the church is to disseminate the message of the gospel and faith, I have chosen to basically write to the "Church" and those who believe. Without question, there are many other definitions or descriptions of this God-ordained institution. For the sake of clarity as the term is addressed in this book, please allow me to share the results of my research which has led me to embrace a working definition.

In the Greek, the word for church is **Ecclesia** which translates "called out" or "those set apart" for God's purpose. Historically, Christians have been referred to as being "set apart," to do the will of God by the unction of the Holy Spirit or by being filled with the Holy Spirit. **Ecclesia** does not exclusively reference Jewish Christians and their religious practices, but the Gentiles as well. The identification of the church is often erroneously relegated to the existence of buildings or physical structures. The original purpose of the church structure, was to provide a place for "the real church" (the believers) to assemble, to worship, and to pray. Jesus asked His disciples a rather pointed and direct question:

"Who do men say that the Son of Man is?" And they said, "Some say John the Baptist; and others Elijah; but still others, Jeremiah or one of the prophets." He said to them, "But who do you say that I am?" Simon Peter answered; you are the Christ, the Son of the living God." And Jesus said unto Peter, 'Blessed are you, Simon Barjona, because flesh and blood did not reveal this to you but my Father who is in heaven. "I also say to you that you are Peter, and upon this rock I will build my Church; and the gates of Hades will not over power it. "I will also give you the keys of the kingdom of heaven; and whatever you bind in earth shall be bound in heaven, and whatever you loose on earth shall be loosed in heaven" **(Matthew 16:13-18).**

Interestingly enough, the only disciple to answer Jesus' question correctly was Peter! Jesus built His Church solely on Peter's statement of faith; and he became the foundation (rock) of the Church because he said, "You are the Christ, Son of the living God." Now it is reasonable then to connect faith to the church. Jesus had no intention of erecting a building. Rather, He sought to establish a spiritual institution of faith.

In order to address its role and function within our spiritual lives, we must first re-visit a general perception of the church. However, it is not a matter of brick and mortar. Regardless of how intricately developed or sophisticated the architecture a building cannot fulfill or contain the spiritual purpose of the church. Nor can it satisfy God's mandate as it relates to the foundation and housing of His Spirit and His will.

The true church is in the hearts of the men and women who believe in God and the soul-sustaining message found in His Word. Simply stated, our faith in Christ is the beginning and the ending of the Church. Unless we, "the called out," believe and demonstrate our faith in God and His Word, the church will not be the godly beacon or institution for the world to see. Without fulfilling this spiritual mandate, the purpose of the "church" is sadly unfulfilled. Faith provides the definitive component upon which the foundation of the church is established. In Peter's second letter to the Church, he wrote:

For it is time for judgment to begin with the household of God; and if it begins with us first, what will be the outcome for those who do not obey the gospel of God? (1 Peter 4:17).

The judgment Peter spoke of is not sin, but our lack of faith in believing God's Word. In the Book of Hebrews the author stated:

"And without faith it is impossible to please Him, for he who comes to God must believe that He is and that He is a rewarder of those who seek Him" (Hebrews 11:6).

The Church holds the keys which unlocks God's power to create the world He desires. God has placed "a measured gift of faith" in EACH of us. Our responsibility as believers is to cultivate that gift of faith into growing evidence of our trust and belief in Him. I believe that this is the greatest time in history for Christians to restore the Church back to its original place of origin and that we the "called out," to 'call in' by Faith, Now, Substance, Hope and with Evidence, the unbeliever into believing the Word of God, His Son and His Holy Spirit.

Introduction

A Day of Total Surrender

It was January 10, 2011 in metropolitan Atlanta. I awakened to an amazingly breathtaking panoramic view of a snowy landscape from my fourth-floor loft apartment overlooking I-285, (the perimeter highway which circles the metro area). The roads were covered with a beautiful blanket-like canvass of white, frozen precipitation which seemed to have completely changed the world I knew.

I had never seen major highways completely immobile! I didn't see a single person, a vehicle, any movement, or any indication of life from my vantage point. At this moment it was simply the snow, my immediate surroundings and me! It's amazing how inclement weather conditions can bring such drastic change to both the appearance of our world and even our perception of that same world.

This change can also alter our mood. It certainly changed mine! It was a surreal moment, as I stood by the window, pondering how life was so fleeting and how the years just kept passing me by. It was as if my life h a d stopped in this moment of time and allowed me to reconnect with the reality of my existence. I was seeing the results of the severe winter storm that was predicted and had left the city and state entrenched in several feet of snow and ice. I stared out the window and listened to the local news stations for what seemed to be several hours reporting the damage caused by the storm and how it would affect travel.

I soon realized the ice was so thick on the roads that driving would be virtually impossible and extremely dangerous. I decided that I would take that time of isolation and reflect on my life.

I turned off the television and sat on my couch. I could not hear a sound other than the rhythmic inhaling and exhaling of my breathing. The stillness became a mystical-gradual-meditative pull that carried me into the abysses of an out-of-body experience. I was in the most peaceful place of serenity I had ever encountered. I spent the next three days inside of my apartment in almost complete silence. Time seemed insignificant as I drifted into the depths of what I knew was a place of infamy for me.

It was a place that I had never been. It was a place that gave me peace. It was a place that forced me into myself, and that caused me to wonder. It was a place where God spoke and I listened. It was a place where I died for the first time. It was a place of my burial; and it was a place of my resurrection. I finally understood what Pastor Wayne C. Thompson of the Fellowship of Faith International Church used to say to me quite often, "Fray White, You need to die to yourself!"

I could never wrap my mind around that concept of dying to myself until that moment in Apartment 8303 in Tucker, GA. It was the day God showed me what it meant to take up my cross and follow Him; to surrender my life totally to His will. I sat on my couch and wept like a new born baby; for it had taken me twenty-eight years to reach a point of death to myself. I immediately started thinking about how my life was all about me and about how my two failed marriages were the result of my deep selfishness and self-centeredness. I thought about the pain I caused both of my ex-wives by going after inconsequential desires and my futile ambitions.

I was never able to balance work and the love they both needed from a husband to feel secure. Men often pride themselves as bearers of material gifts when the greatest of all gifts should be Christ, love, and quality time. Christ must be the scale and the measuring instrument for any successful marriage. Only when God reveals to you the errors of your ways can you really see what His plans are for the family. That place with Him exposed my many paths as those of a broad and destructive journey. It was the most introspective and self-examination I had ever taken of myself. In a flash of historical reviews, I could see and even hear some of the arguments of both wives saying, "You don't spend enough time with me!" They were both correct!

I reflected on how I equated material possessions with love. I could not stop weeping as I cried thinking about how my children missed so much while I chased after my desires to build a business and life that had ended two marriages. I fought back the tears that seemingly flowed for hours. I eventually wept myself into a peaceful rest and lay across the couch staring at the ceiling. I knew I could not continue down that same path of meaningless expectations and futile ambitions. As time passed the quietness allowed my inner thoughts to consume me with truth. I stood up again by the window and continued to observe the sheer beauty and mystical wonders of the divine winter storm. Accumulation of snow and ice in the Atlanta area creates hazardous conditions of major proportions.

Many times, as in this instance, these ice storms are responsible for a shut-down of the entire region. Usually there are only a few days of snow and ice in the area so there isn't a real need for local municipalities to invest in millions of dollars of snow and ice-removal equipment. Except for clearing major transportation arteries, the rest is left to melt away with the return of the sun. Therefore, these brief periods of snow and ice create an un-scheduled winter break of sorts for the general population.

It took isolation, and a snow and ice storm to bring me closer to personal destiny and to move in the faith required to honor God's will for my life. Until this moment, I had many distractions; too many!

This sudden wintry interruption of my regular activity placed me squarely before God and painfully exposed my ill-chosen path and destructive journey. Determined to make right a wrong, I purposed to begin a new phase of my life. There were many bridges to re- build, bad habits to break, yet, there was still time to submit to a life which reflected the will of God for me. Even though there is absolutely nothing wrong with being successful, God had not created me to be the most dynamic and highly recognized businessman on earth—certainly not at the sacrifice of my family.

Before anyone had the opportunity to think of creating a business, God created man, gave him a garden to tend (job) and wisely gave him a wife for companionship (helper). He then made them a family. Productivity, wealth and enterprise must not take precedence over God, marriage or family, but we must live a balanced life in order to thrive successfully. After a few days, the storm subsided, the ice melted and the city returned to normal.

As I ventured out to rejoin civilization, my goal was to live and prioritize differently. The intimate encounter with God had proven that He should be at the center of my existence as well as the orchestrator of my new identity. I needed to give up the baton and place it in His hands. I submitted to biblical teaching under several tremendous spiritual leaders. I also sought spiritual counsel. I was determined that the new Fray would be a better man, much better than most businessmen could ever be. Success was still a part of my dream however, not at the sake of balance and obedience to God's commands. I hope somewhere there is a husband or a wife, a father or a mother, who might presently be more involved in achieving success than reigning as the true godly priest or priestess of their home reading my story.

I also hope that my experience will be a part of re-evaluation of your purpose and methods so that your loved one's lives will not be negatively affected. After much soul-searching and praying before God, mending my ways and following His instruction, I was inspired to become transparent and share my story. I hope it will serve as a catalyst for others who stand in the need of direction and want to believe in His ways, but perhaps lack the knowledge to go forward. This book is for you. The journey has been complex, sometimes joyful and at other times equally sorrowful because our past mistakes tend to haunt us through the years, especially as we press to move forward. In spite of it all, I would take nothing for my journey.

It has brought me to this point and positioned me to speak with relative authority. I started thinking about this book and the title and how to best share my story. To solidify my vision, I initiated the process of publishing by registering the title through securing an ISBN number. This was accomplished without any real problem. I decided the title would be, "Now... Faith Is..."

I then considered the sub-title:

How to Create the Life You Desire to Live by
Faith and by Works (Action)

Later, I wondered if the subtitle could possibly mislead readers. I did not want to have any part in leading anyone to the pitfalls of self-aggrandizement which could lead to the "its-all-about-me" syndrome. It is actually never about YOU; rather it is all about GOD! I realized that I had lived the life I desired and now I felt its impact. For my effort, I had experienced only emptiness in contrast to the life God originally desired for me. I knew that if anyone read this book without my pointing them specifically to God and His way that I would be personally responsible for misguiding him or her to a place of potential failure.

I immediately called the publishing company from which I had acquired my ISBN number to inquire about changing my subtitle. The representative told me that I could change the subtitle as long as I had not published the book. I grabbed my computer and made the change. Thank you, God for "point and click!" I felt immediate relief and assurance as I entered the new subtitle. Immediately, I felt redeemed and relieved with the change:

"How to Create the Life **God** Desires for You to Live by Faith and by Works (Actions)

I was totally convinced that the life I had chosen for myself was not the life God had desired for me, and I was willing to start anew, but would begin by first seeking God's desire with all of my heart. I thought about how so many of my friends and fellow business owners were losing their families and possessions. I also realized that many of our problems were similar in nature. We were ill-focused and had lived unbalanced lives.

God has allowed me by His grace to experience an extremely interesting and eventful life. I have traveled to numerous places around the world, owned successful businesses, have lived in large houses, owned fancy automobiles, made large sums of money, met important people, and enjoyed what some would describe as the finer things of life. Yet, in the midst of it all, for a long time my existence was very empty. Foolishly, I thought "things" would complete me; but they did not.

Today, I am a living witness that all of these pleasures and material gain yield absolutely nothing but disappointment if they are not a part of God's desire for your life or not appropriately aligned with His will. It is my prayer that this book will challenge you and lead you through the process of living the life God desires for you. However, you must first have that "death" experience. Perhaps you are thinking as I said to Pastor Thompson.

"I've been through an awful lot already. I thought I had died!" However, if you are not at a place of death to yourself, you will never experience that Genesis moment when God will say, "Let there be!" God has to take you to that place of death, burial, and resurrection—where it is dark and formless and His Holy Spirit awaits His command to say: "Let there be light!"

I promise you the revelation from God for your life will spring forth from this experience. There is no greater place of beginning than to surrender fully one's life back into the hands from where it started. It is a Divine experience when the "creation" finally yields to the Creator! Our initial relationship or walk with the Creator began in total darkness and will end in total light through His Son, Christ!!

Faith in Darkness into the MarvelousLight

In the Book of Genesis, Moses wrote: In the beginning God created the heavens and the earth was without form and void; and darkness was upon the face of the deep and the Spirit of God moved upon the face of the waters. And God said, "Let there be light, and there was light" (Genesis 1:1-3). God spoke everything He imagined into existence to remain from generation to generation.

Truth: God is trans-generational...

This six-day process completely changed the course of a darkened past and brought forth an imminent future of light, life, sustenance, and the abundance of *possibilities* for every living creature to thrive, recreate, and to enjoy.

The word Genesis means origin, beginning, start, and birth. God *created* the heavens and earth from total darkness, formlessness and void. God's creation should encourage you to believe that you do not need a thing to create the life God desires for you except *(faith, vision, and action).* Presently, you may consider this moment to be dark and formless, but it is not! I am here to tell you that this is your finest hour. I said, "This is your finest hour!"

It is in this dark and formless place that *dreams, ideas, visions, meditations* and *thoughts* are given to you by God to elevate your imagination into transforming divine *revelations* and *inspirations* into reality.

We often see and hear these two powerful infinite words often, but we never grasp the true essence of their meanings. The word *revelation* is exposure, disclosure, leak, admission, surprise, and shock. When God reveals His visions these words are some of His methods of communicating those visions to us.

Inspiration has a variety of meanings that are tantamount with the attributes and power of God: stimulus, spur, motivation, encouragement, muse and more importantly, creativity.

The Bible is a book of God inspired messages, stories and events written about God, Jesus, the Holy Spirit, men and women who trusted and believed what was spoken to them by Him. As a matter of fact, some of our greatest inventions, ideas, and God inspired purposes have been discovered when people were in their perceived darkest and formless moments. Creative images are produced by revelations from God to challenge us within when we are in our perceived darkness.

In essence, an image (revelation) can be birthed against a dark, blank or formless background. Pictures are developed in the dark, **movies** are shown in the dark, and visions and dreams are profound during our sleep. A **Dream** is defined as a series of images, ideas, emotions, and sensations occurring involuntarily in the mind during certain stages of sleep. The author of the New Testament book Matthew described the perceived darkest hours of Jesus' life and the glory Jesus received afterwards, he wrote:

Now from the <u>sixth hour</u> there was darkness fell all over the land until the ninth hour. And about the <u>ninth hour</u> Jesus cried with a loud voice, saying, E'li, E'li, la-ma'ma sa-bach'-tha-ni, That is to say, My God, My God why have you forsaken me?
(Matthew 27:45-46, emphasis with underline mine).

Coincidentally, the number *six represents* the creation of man, and the **nine** the power of the Holy Spirit, fruit of the spirit, and divine completeness (biblical time for the *sixth-hour* is 12:00 pm. and the *ninth-hour* is 3:00 pm.). The Bible describes the tearing of the veil in the temple of God from top to bottom. His death gives us direct access to God through Him. We no longer need a priest to pray or bring sacrifices for our sins: We can now come boldly to His Throne of Grace, in "Jesus" Name!

The Bible says:

At that moment, the Temple curtain was ripped in two, top to bottom. There was an earthquake, and rocks were split in pieces. What's more, tombs were opened up, and many bodies of believers asleep in their graves were raised. After Jesus' resurrection, they left the tombs, entered the holy city, and appeared to many (**Matthew 27:51-53**).

Jesus' death liberated and gave us direct access to a whole new way of life and laid the foundation for eternal salvation. In your darkest moment, God is developing you and the exposures (pictures) of the vision He has for your life. You **will** begin to see these images gradually become vivid revelations of your future and the many possibilities that await you. As the people witnessed Jesus hanging on the cross at Calvary in total darkness, they began **seeing** the true revelation, image, and power of God.

Now when the Centurion, and those who were with him keeping guard over Jesus, when they saw the earthquake and the things that were happening, became very frightened and said, "Truly this was the Son of God!" (**Matthew 27:45-54**).

The apostle Paul wrote of the power we will receive through Christ's death. He said:

"For indeed He was crucified because of weakness, yet He lives because of the power of God. For we are also weak in Him, yet we will live with Him because of the power of God directed towards you" (2 Corinthians 13:4).

Our **perceived** death, burial, and resurrection will likewise release the **Faith** God placed within each of us. We **must** affect the lives of those we encounter and take them into the liberty that Christ intended for them to love, live, and lead in. The very first principle of **Faith** is to **Believe that Christ is the Son of God!**

The second is to **FOLLOW CHRIST!**

This principle is the greatest test of our Christian experience. Scripture proves that if we follow Christ He will show us our divine purpose, He states it plainly:

Now as Jesus was walking by the Sea of Galilee, He saw two brothers, Simon who was called Peter, and Andrew his brother, casting a net into the sea; for they were fishermen. And He said to them, "Follow Me, and I will make you fishers of men." Immediately they left their nets and followed Him (Matthew 4:18-19).

Following Christ

Jesus said, "You didn't chose me, but I chose you!" (John 15:16) He told Peter, "I will make you fishers of men." Jesus will tell you exactly what you will be if you follow Him long enough and endure the persecution and process to see the full manifestation of his calling for your life. Most people hear the call, but miss the choosing. The calling requires total commitment to what He tells you to do. It will change your life forever and you will change other lives forever. Most people never truly commit to this moment, so I will ASK you, will <u>You</u> follow Christ? If you say yes, you have just found your purpose in life. It's a promise from God.

The third principle is to **SERVE!** Jesus' primary assignment was to serve a world that did not know or love Him. You can literally serve your way into favor, and favor brings opportunity, and opportunity can bring prosperity in every area of your life.

True serving, sets in motion a spiritual principle (LAW) understood only by those who have an intimate encounter, relationship and experience with God. In the third book of the New Testament, Luke wrote:

"Then they began to argue among themselves about who would be the greatest among them. Jesus told them, "In this world the kings and great men lord it over their people, yet they are called, "friends of the people." But among you it will be different. Those who are the greatest among you should take the lowest rank, and the leader should be like the servant. Who is more important, the one who sits at the table or the one who serves? The one who sits at the table, of course. But not here! For I am among you as one who serves"
(Luke: 22:24-27).

Jesus' greatness came from His willingness to serve, and so will yours. We find ourselves in perceived **darkness only** when we cease from serving others. True prosperity is a by-product of serving and providing a service that enhances the lives of a multiplicity of people.

Life is a numbers game! If you are not positively affecting the lives of others, you **will** fall into selfishness and become self-serving, thereby cutting off your ability for consistent opportunity and favor. Mainly because, your whole existence revolves around your needs, consuming every thought with only one person in mind... YOU!

Serving is a basic concept of faith; it will work for you if you work it! A life of serving culminates into joy and peace, knowing that serving is never about you, for the ultimate purpose of serving is to present 'Christ' as the foundation of faith. Serving others releases the creativity out of the individual and causes an outpouring of goodwill and recognition. Lastly, serving will expand your area of influence, privileges, and trustworthiness.

Serving Others

Create a list of the names of six people, organizations, or institutions you will begin serving and **MOVE** into the marvelous light. As you serve your way out of darkness (or present state) into the liberty in Christ, you will discover a new purpose in **LOVE** for others. If you are unemployed or underemployed seek a place to serve earnestly in an arena you desire to work in. This is why internships are so successful to those who participate and serve. Usually the organizations will create a position or refer you to another company if they see you are a good server.

Keep Following Christ and Serving Others

In Perceived DARKNESS to the Light in Christ

JESUS   THE CHRIST
_____   _____

SAUL   THE APOSTLE PAUL
_____   _____

FRAY   THE FATHER / MINISTER
_____   _____

_____   _____

One of the greatest examples of this principle working was taught and demonstrated by a contemporary of Dr. Martin Luther King Jr. He said, "The best way to find yourself is to lose yourself in the service of others." **Mahatma Gandhi**

Serving takes all of the focus off your *perceived* darkness or present state and places a responsibility and obligation on you to present a new life of love in the *now* to these individuals through your *faith* in serving.

For example, Jesus and Saul served people and led them to a whole *new* way of life. They also revealed to the people they served a completely *new* identity, purpose and destiny. Serving changes the attitude and altitude of you and the people you serve. It's an open invitation into a vast world of immeasurable favor. The act of godly serving invokes the law of reciprocity meaning, you have released the power and glory of God to bless and promote you.

Now that you've written your six names (Family first), pray that God uses your *serving* to expose and develop the gifts that are resident and lying dormant inside of you. The word "sell" derives from the Scandinavian root "**selzig**," which means "**server**." We must acknowledge that we are all sellers. You are a seller and server! Henry Ford, founder of Ford Motor Company said, "Wealth, like happiness, is never attained when sought after directly. It comes as a by-product of providing a useful service."

Fact: Nothing happens in this world until someone sells something. You must become a great sales person. It's the highest paid profession in all industries.

The following tips are a few simple principles of serving:

- To serve, the person's needs and wants must be priority and met.

- To determine their needs, you must ask and be open to fulfilling their request joyfully and timely.

- Always want them to have the very best. Listen and write down the details.

- Be sure to give them exactly what they want plus more, with a spirit of excellence and humility.

- Always follow-up after each task to confirm acceptance and satisfaction.

- Never feel that you are doing them a favor, but convey to them that to serve them is an honor.

We are all sellers in some capacity. Everything we do in life is a form of selling. You are exactly where you are for lack of serving or because you sell yourself and provide a service needed by the individuals you serve. You are compensated solely to the degree that you meet the needs and wants of the one's you are serving. Professionally, if you serve in low paying industries, you will be compensated accordingly. If you serve in high paying industries, the job will yield equal or greater compensation.

You can also incorporate these same principles and serving practices when you have faith enough to start your own business. Ideally, your goal should be to transition your serving into some form of entrepreneurship. Therefore, you must stay relevant through training and continual educational programs in order to grow and serve in arenas that compensate you well. Serving God and His Church has exponential return factors that cannot be measured.

A Word of Caution to Church Leaders

Church leaders should be extremely conscious and responsible of how they utilize their server's time and effort. Their ministries should illustrate spiritual accountability. All leaders must not allow individuals who serve them to neglect their families and personal obligations through excessively serving their ministries. Moreover, they should never use them for personal gain or abuse them because of their willingness to serve and satisfy the leaders. I have personally witnessed this misuse of influence and lack of consideration for the server's sincere zeal, love, enthusiasm to serve.

Leaders must help manage their server's time and be aware of the server's personal responsibilities and commitments outside of their ministry by simply inquiring periodically. Every ministry should implement balanced scheduling for servers, to insure that all leaders are equally aware and concerned mutually, so that serving becomes a pleasant experience in each ministry. Finally, love is the fuse which when lit, will ignite the power of God to truly administer the grace and mercy needed to serve in the ministry of Jesus Christ.

Oftentimes, it takes our perceived darkest and formless experience for God to show forth our purpose on earth. Remember, Jesus went into total darkness, but God empowered Him with His Holy Spirit, and after three days, He was raised as "The Christ."

God sent Jesus here as a *Gift* to be planted in the deepest depths of hell in order to release and totally eradicate the effects of eternal damnation. His death buries our old life and sets in motion a world of **new beginnings**. In this new beginning, you will be liberated and transformed into Jesus' marvelous image of light, and given His divine heavenly power, literally enabling you to change every perceived and darkened circumstance into a positive, life-giving experience through faith and your creativity.

Creativity Starts in Darkness

It was in that darkness that God created the heavens and earth.

It was in that darkness that God put Adam to sleep and created Eve.

It was in that darkness, that Abel's blood spoke to God.

It was in that dark, smelly, and lonely ark that Noah and his family endured forty days and forty nights of pounding rain on their way to a new beginning.

It was in that darkness and with a feeling of the unknown that God said, "Leave your country and go to a better place I have for you!" And at seventy-five years of age, Abram and Sarai obeyed, and God called Abraham "His friend!"

It was in that darkness that God tested Abraham and in the morning, he arose to sacrifice his son Isaac.

It was in that darkness that Jacob deceived his father Isaac and stole Esau's birthright (part of God's plan).

It was in that darkness that Jacob wrestled with the Angel of Lord and became Israel.

It was in that darkness of a dream that Joseph saw his brothers bowing down to him.

It was in that darkness of a pit that Joseph ended up in Potiphar's house (King of Egypt).

It was in that darkness of a prison that Joseph became governor of Egypt.

It was in that dark and 'backside of the dessert' (meaning adversity) that God spoke to Moses from the burning bush.

It was under the pillar of fire that God provided the Israelites light to travel through the darkness on their journey through the wilderness into (the Promise Land).

It was after the darkness of the death of Moses that God told Joshua, his servant to, "Arise and go over to this Jordan."

It was in that darkness that the prostitute Rahab, lied and hid the two Israelites sent by Moses to spy out Jericho (the Promised Land)). And through her faith and lineage came Jesus and our subsequent salvation.

It was in that darkness of the Cave of Adullam that David transformed four-hundred distressed, dejected, in-debt and troubled men into mighty men of valor.

It was in that darkness of a vision from the angel of the Lord that Isaiah heard God ask, "Whom should I send as a messenger to this people?" "Who will go for us?" That Isaiah said to the Lord; "Here I am. Send me."

It was in that darkness of the womb of Jeremiah's mother that God said, "And before you were born I consecrated you; I appointed you a prophet unto the nations."

It was in that darkness of over 400 years between The Old Testament and The New Testament that God did not speak to His prophets or people, but He would soon usher in the 'Light of the World' through His Son Jesus the Christ.

It was in that darkness that and angel of the Lord appeared to him in a dream and said. "Joseph, son of David, do not be afraid to take Mary as your wife. For the child with her was conceived by the Holy Spirit. And she will have a son, and you are to name him Jesus, for he will save his people from their sin."

It was in that darkness of the womb of Elizabeth that John the Baptist leaped when Mary entered her house impregnated by the Holy Spirit, with the Son of God in her womb.

It was in that darkness that wise men met the angel of the Lord radiant with light that told them, "Go to Bethlehem to see the Son of God lying in a manger."

It was in that darkness from the six hour until the ninth hour that Jesus died for our sins.

It was in that darkness of three days in hell that Jesus defeated Satan (death) and released us from eternal damnation and became the Christ.

The apostle Paul wrote about Jesus' experience in his letter to the Romans, clearly saying:

"Or do you not know that all of us who have been baptized into Christ Jesus have been baptized into His death? Therefore we have been buried with Him through baptism into death, so that as Christ was raised from the dead through the glory of the Father, so we too might walk in newness of life" **(Romans 6:3-4)**.

Lastly, it is in this dark and formless place of *prayer*, *communion* and *truth*, with truth meaning: YOUR DEATH, YOUR BURIAL, YOUR DEAD-END; THE END of YOURSELF, and A TOTAL SURRENDERING POINT TO GOD that you are RESSURECTED in CHRIST!

I pray that you stop and reason with God, *now*, before you read another page of this book. I pray your heart is pure, and after careful consideration and thought, you ask God for a true and divine encounter with Christ. If you sincerely surrender today and now... this day, becomes the day you will discover God's newness, His ordained plan, and His purpose for your life.

God uses this dark and formless experience as an appointed time of revelation, inspiration, and impartation maturation and brands you as His willing servant. He strips away all that is not Him. He breaks OUR will, He prunes and He burns off all of our imperfections. He prepares us for His service as representatives of His Word and His kingdom.

He strengthens us, builds our character, and exposes and forgives every hidden secret of sin with His marvelous light in Christ. Your spirit will become humble, obedient, contrite, repentant, forgiving, and love will become primary in your willingness to live a mirror image of Christ. We become *gifts* that He uses to present to the world the exciting possibilities of living a life of faith in Him.

We should welcome God with open arms and excitement. Some of us, however, might mistake this darkness as Him having forsaken them, when to the contrary; He has *fore-taken* us into a new dimension that we have never seen or imagined, and through this darkness, He presents to us the *Screen-play* and *Motion picture* of our *New lives, identity, purpose* and *destiny*.

Chapter One
It All Starts With Prayer and Meditation...

Our world is in a state of absolute disarray and mass confusion. We are bombarded with radio, television, cell phones, iPads, Nooks, Kindles, iPhones, media, Internet, automated billboards, and constant communication from all spheres of life. It is virtually impossible to stay connected to God with the amount of distractions *we* allow to interfere with our prayer and meditation time—our relationship with God. We are inundated perpetually with streams of man-made data flowing endlessly into the receptors of our minds. How can we find time for prayer and meditation?

The companies that create these multi-media audio and visual companions to us have become dictates, appealing to the psyche of our futures. We have visual information displays in supermarket lines, bathrooms, hotel lobbies, service stations, planes, trains, buses, and everywhere else imaginable. We have given these companies and advertisers direct access into the most inner-being of our minds and allow the information, whether erroneous or accurate, to shape our thinking and form our belief systems. We have so many electronic devices and companies competing for our minds, loyalty-of-brand, and attention that our prayer lives have become tireless efforts of subtle gratitude toward God.

Unfortunately, our society have become dependently engrossed in these gadgets and companies as life-enhancers when, to the contrary, they have become little idols of distractions. I found myself being co-dependent on these *time* and *creativity* robbers as their companies' messages continue to invade my thoughts and interrupt my peace and tranquility during the day and often at night. Many of us cannot sit in a quiet environment or room for any length of time without having one or more of these devices turned on.

Prayer once ruled these revered moments. It was a time of divine impartation from the Most High God, and our homes were formerly center stage where miracles of His existence reigned. Now these electronic gadgets have become major points of emphasis in our society and have created a subconscious-epidemic of dependency that we must begin to classify as addictions.

They shape our desires and send their words through subliminal marketing tactics that hinder our ability to pray for divine revelation. They have replaced the sacred time we once reserved for prayer, meditation and from hearing instructions and directions from God. In other words, we deprive ourselves from a true commitment to intimacy, prayer and meditation with God.

Prayer has become an abandoned choice of ritualistic gestures, reserved only for special circumstances and unexpected chaotic events that require supernatural interventions from God. God is not going to compete with these multi-media devices and companies that **we** have allowed to replace Him as the source of revelation, inspiration, and creativity while omitting prayer and meditation from our daily lives. ...

God always searches the heart of a man or woman in prayer. He chooses people to effect change on the earth when they are enthusiastic about His cause, for He knows they will have singleness of purpose. If you follow the progress of individuals who consistently pray, they are rarely diverted by external forces that rob them of their time, passion and commitment to prayer and meditation. They are able to remain focused on the vision they receive from God and are not distracted by temporary interruptions from people or audio-visual distracters.

I have taken the liberty to list below some 'Gadget Makers' and 'Advertisers' themes to awaken you to the power of the campaigns of companies that promises to lead you into destiny and future. The advertising and technological devices these companies use as so-called *divine messaging* become obsolete in a matter of months, if not weeks! God's Word, however, will never become out dated. Through prayer, meditation and His word, He will enrich and change every circumstance imaginable... Always!

Please read these man-made slogans that are shaping the very way we live and leading us down a short road of disappointment and despair and compare them to the last company's (God's) promise.

Panasonic

Ideas for life: Panasonic generates ideas for life... today and tomorrow. Through innovative thinking, we are committed to enriching people's lives around the world.

Sony USA

Believe that anything you imagine, you can make real.

SAMSUNG

Imagine what **Samsung** can do for you!

AT&T

Your World. Delivered

BellSouth

Listening, Answering

Nokia
Connecting People

7-Eleven

Oh Thank Heaven for 7-Eleven

Yahoo!

Your World. Your Way.
Yahoo! makes it easy to enjoy what matters most in your
world.

Verizon Wireless

"Can you hear me now? Good."

God: The Holy Bible

"Call To Me and I Will Answer and Tell You Great and
Mighty Things Which You Do Not Know" **(Jeremiah 33:3)**.

When Christ answers, there will be no mistake whether it's an electronic gadget, advertising or a heavenly call. Your life will be interrupted divinely and oftentimes, suddenly! The divine assignment from God usually connects you with human intervention instructed from Him to validate His response to your call. He used a fellow Christian Brother, Ananias to deliver His message to Saul while he was praying.

God's Vision in Prayer and Meditation

The notorious Christian persecutor, Saul, is a classic example of how God will reach out and touch the one He calls. Saul was on the road to Damascus to deliver a new order from Jewish leaders authorizing the continuation of persecution to Christian believers when suddenly, the 'Light of Christ' was so bright that it changed his life forever.

The Book of Acts records this event in detail:

As he was traveling, it happened that he was approaching Damascus, and suddenly a light from heaven flashed around him; and he fell to the ground and heard a voice saying to him; Saul, Saul, why are you persecuting Me?" And he said, "Who are you, Lord?" And He said, "I am Jesus whom you are persecuting, but get up and enter the city, and it will be told you what you must do" (Act9:3-6).

The Bible states Saul was in total darkness for three straight days after being blinded by the Light of Christ and being in the presence of God. It further records that Saul was *praying* and did not eat or drink.

While *praying*, he received a **vision** that he might receive his sight by the laying on of hands from Ananias. The Scriptures gives explicit details of what occurred.

5

The apostle Luke wrote the following: *"And the Lord said unto him," Get up and go to the street called Straight, and inquire at the house of Judas for a man from Tarsus named Saul, for he is praying,and he has seen in a vision a man name Ananias come in and lay hands on him, so that he might regain his sight"* **(Acts:11-12).**

Saul totally shut the world off for a one on one encounter with God. He had no idea what he was about to become. After this spiritual intervention, Saul became the Apostle Paul. Saul got a vision as he prayed. Visions are one of the ways you will get your revelations and inspirations. Prayer and meditation is the key that unlocks the future of each of our destinies. Will you, like Saul, allow the "Light of Christ" to change your life, or will you continue to be led down the road of obsolescence and disappointment by technology or other distractions or will you pray and call on God?

True prayer closes all doors of distraction from every direction except heaven. It creates a direct spiritual line of communication between you and Christ who sits at the right hand of the "Throne of God" interceding for you. Through prayer and meditation, He keeps us moving forward, balanced, and focused on the vision and methodology for attaining the vision. God will always answer you in His perfect time and intimate manner.

He will always validate what He tells you with His Word or by some divine method or godly person. The Bible must be your navigational system as you disconnect from daily prayer and meditation. God's Word will always invalidate the doubt that you will encounter as you move from hope unseen to the evidence of reality. It is vitality important that you maintain consistent connectivity through prayer and meditation on Him.

For He will continue downloading essential information needed until you have manifested what was agreed upon by His vision for your life. He will never give you something too big in the beginning until you have proven your ability to obtain and maintain it adequately. He is the foundation of any endeavor.

In essence, the very act of incorporating God into your plans will bring Him on board as 'The Chairman' to have the final word in all decisions. His impartation of directions will come through His Spirit and through man in a series of revelations, inspirations and cooperation as your faith to believe grows. Each impartation increases and is · relegated by YOUR ability to move forward by faith in what He has revealed to you.

Will you have that **one** on **one** encounter with God and **move** into your purpose and destiny? Prayer and meditation aligns our mind to the godly capacity to create anything that God desires. Unfortunately, most people exclude these vital components and neglect these intimate moments as paths of clarity to major opportunity, greatness, and guaranteed success.

Coincidently, the closing of our eyes in prayer and meditation is a form of darkness and formlessness. Prayer is the spiritual-connecting-mechanism for man to coexist between Christ and God. It produces an atmosphere of truth conducive to hear what God is saying to you. Meditation is the corresponding after-effect of God to an earnest heart-purging individual prostrating themselves in sincere search of His instructions and guidance.

What will you become from your dark or formless hour or present state? Will you pray today, meditate and call on God? What a wonderful opportunity to share intimacy with God in prayer, meditation and the intercession of Christ and be led by His Holy Spirit!

7

"Therefore He is able to save forever those that draw near to God through Him since He always lives to make intercession for them" **(Hebrews 7:25)**.

From Abraham, to Moses, to Christ, and to every great man or woman of God in biblical, historical or modern day, they all had or have one thing in common, ***prayer*** and ***meditation!*** God is the core source of power to all of our needs and desires. If you are in a state of flux, and you do not have a vision or a solution to a problem, it is in this very act of communication (prayer and meditation) with God that He will begin fellowship with you.

The apostle John wrote: *"For God is Spirit so those that worship Him must worship Him in spirit and in truth"* **(John 4:24)**.

Truth being, I've resolved to a fact that when I don't have an answer to a concern, God will provide one as I commune with Him. There is not an occasion when I have come sincerely to God to minister and meditate on Him or with a challenge that He does not give me an answer. His answers are usually never as I think they should be. His ways are indeed higher than ours! Isaiah the prophet confirmed this truth when he so eloquently wrote God's statement to him saying:

"For My thoughts are not your thoughts, nor are your ways My ways," *declares the Lord. "For as the heavens are higher than the earth, so are My ways higher than your ways and my thoughts than your thoughts"* **(Isaiah 55:8-9)**.

Usually through meditating on God after prayer, His answers or solutions come in a peaceful series of impartations and never the way I predicted or from whom I imagined. Webster defines meditation as: a written or spoken discourse expressing considered thoughts on a subject.

Prayer and meditation in truth are the most powerful forms of communication on earth. They transcend time zones, speeds, and distances with absolute precision of destination. We don't need satellites, microwaves, laser beams, cells phones, the Internet, carrier pigeons, notes in bottle, a wagon train, or the Pony Express to deliver our message. We must come in spirit and truth and close with "In Jesus Name"... Amen!

Prayer is the least expensive, but most effective, method of spiritual communication with God known to man. Without prayer, the foundation of our faith has no basis for direction or clarity. **Note:** All godly and trans- generational ideas will come from God. Ideas are thoughts, notions, concepts, designs, wisdom, thinking, and planning. When *He* gives you a vision as I stated earlier, it is never bigger than what you can handle, but it will require **constant contact** for Supreme guidance.

This divine and spiritual discernment will come by revelation or inspiration through the Holy Spirit. The Bible describes many of the prophets receiving their revelation or inspiration as the following:

"Then the angel of the Lord appeared to him in a blazing fire" (**Moses, Exodus 3:2**).

"For thus the word spoke to me with mighty power and instructed me not to walk in the way of this people saying," (**Isaiah, 8:11**).

"Now the word of Lord came to me saying," (**Jeremiah, 1:4**).

"The Lord said to me," (**Ezekiel, 44:5**).

"While I was still speaking in prayer, then the man Gabriel, whom I had seen in the vision previously, came to me in my extreme weariness about the time of the evening offering. He gave me instruction and talked with me and said, "O Daniel, I have now come forth to give you

insight with understanding. *"At the beginning of your supplication the command was issued, and I have come down to tell you for you are highly esteemed; so give heed to the message and gain understanding of the vision"* **(Daniel 9:21-22).**

God has not changed His methods of communication He can speak in any form He desires and send whomever to deliver the vision. However, what initiates the process is prayer. Usually, the moment we start praying, if our hearts are pure, He begins instructing and constructing the plans for our lives no matter where we find ourselves.

Create a Place for Prayer

The first account of an altar (a high sacred place designated for prayer and sacrifice) is in the Book of Genesis:

Then Noah built an altar to the LORD, and took every clean animal and every clean bird and offered burnt offerings on the altar. The LORD smelled the soothing aroma; and the LORD said to Himself, " I will never again curse the ground on account of man, for the intent of man's heart is evil from his youth; and I will never again destroy every living thing as I had done **(Genesis 8:20-21).**

You should create an altar in your home, closet (Refer to Matthew 6:9-15) or any place you desire and deem it sacred. God sees the heart and intentions. I have been told by many of my friends that in their prayer rooms they can feel the presence of God when they enter it. I have a place where I commune with God, and I find it is holy and empowering. In my intimate moments of communion and meditation, I get downloads and strategies needed for my endeavors and impartations of information usually pertaining to things that I have not asked for or happened yet, but I believe they will.

I know it is God giving me insight of things in which He plans to prosper me in. In the Book of Joshua, He even commanded Joshua to meditate, be strong and courageous. Meditating on God's Word removes the fear that often accompanies the unknown.

God was very direct when He spoke to Joshua, saying:

"This book of the Law shall not depart from your mouth, but you shall meditate on it day and night, so that you maybe careful to do according to all that is written in it; for then you shall make your way prosperous, and then you will have good success" **(Joshua 1:8)**.

The opportunity to meditate and commune with God should be an amazingly exciting experience of spiritual rejuvenation and unparalleled each time we encounter His presence.

We should press deeper for a different level of intimacy and not settle for the previous exchange of grace and power. He wants us to have strength and courage as we connect with Him. God concluded His directives to Joshua by saying:

"Have I not commanded you? Be strong and courageous! Do not tremble or be dismayed, for I will be with you wherever you go!" **(Joshua 1:9)**.

The moment you understand that the presence of God is with you; there is nothing that can hold you back or intimidate you. Prayer and meditation connects you to the mind of God and transitions you into faith, which gives you the confidence that what has been revealed to you will happen. He provides the blueprint and clarity to accomplish it by the divine impartations received during this precious time you have dedicated in prayer and meditation with Him.

Prayer and Meditation
Connects You to the Mind of God

The mind of God is always forward moving and inspiring. He never dwells on the past nor does He want us living in our past mistakes. Jesus expressed this rather plainly in his letter to the Philippians, saying:

"Let this mind be in you which was also in Christ Jesus Who, being in the form of God, thought it not robbery to be equal with God: But made himself of no reputation, and took upon him the form of a servant, and was made in the likeness of men: And being found in fashion as a man, he humbled himself, and became obedient unto death, even the death of the cross" **(Philippians 2:5-8)**.

Having the mind of Christ requires that we have a spiritual death of this world's thinking and adopt the spiritual mind of Christ and all that His death represents, which is a full life of abundant living in the kingdom of God. Whatever place you find yourself at this moment— good, bad or indifferent is the life you have created, allowed to be created, or have accepted. This existence is a direct result of what you have allowed to be formulated in your mind.

The mind is one of the most power tools on earth. It is more powerful than the hydrogen bomb! It is more powerful than the atomic bomb! It is more powerful than any nuclear bomb known or will ever be known to man. Why? Because the mind is what created these weapons of mass ***destruction!*** Just as it has the capacity to destroy, the mind has an even greater capacity to create weapons of mass ***construction!***

The mind was not created to dwell on or in the past or future, because its general purpose focuses on the NOW! Any other direction either past or present renders it void . It cannot predict what the future holds, because it only works in the present. Only God can tell you what is going to happen past today. However, His trans-generational plans for our lives are divinely given. I don't know anyone living the life they expected, planned or didn't experience the reality of the unpredictability in our future since the 2008 crisis.

Man will never see his plans fully materialize without the presence of God; regardless of how finitely detailed they are. In essence, it's okay to plan for the future, but only God truly knows for certain the outcome. The mind is continuously stimulated by new images and ideas. It does not function at optimum capability when it is *recycling* old experiences.

Conversely, past negative thoughts causes the mind to cease valuable thought patterns of progressive data and re- sift through the historical review of unnecessary trivial garbage that should have been discarded as useless and obsolete. The mind thrives when new information and revelations are constantly feeding it to produce flowing impulses of divine creativity. The second we connect to the mind of God, He presents our mind with fresh visions, thoughts, suggestions, and plans.

It begins to process and deduce the information strategically with a positive force of persuasion. It is only when we **doubt** His vision or move ahead of Him that we falter in OUR efforts and descend into disappointment and despair. You must *never* allow fear or doubt to change the initial image! If you can maintain (in meditation) the revelation from God for any period of time, it can never be erased from the mind.

These positive imprints given to you by God become embedded as occupants of the mind. They require daily rations of creative ideas and thoughts *encircling* the image *(not recycling)* to produce the very object of desire. At any moment you can stop and have an "And God said..." revelation during prayer and meditation that will change your life and the lives of generations to follow.

As stated earlier, "God is a trans-generational" *(forward moving Creator)* and He expects us to be the same. His imagination created the heavens and earth. Just imagine removing every single man-created object, edifice, or invention from the face of the earth. It would give you a slight idea of what God originally created. Oh! How marvelous His earth is and all of its beauty: the sun, the moon, the stars, the ocean, the flowers, the birds, the trees, the rain, and more importantly... Man! At best, we can only add to the aesthetics that compliment and accentuate His divine universal architecture.

He laid the foundation and wants us to build upon it. He expects us to create these marvelous things in this *present* dispensation of time to balance His creation, to give Him glory, to promote man's welfare; and to exist for our enjoyment. When God created man in His own image and likeness, He placed him on earth and gave him the same ability to create.

He said, "Be fruitful, multiply, replenish, and dominate" (Genesis 1:28). Basically, saying: create generationally! Let's examine the second verse in Genesis. The Bible clearly states, "And the Spirit of God was moving (encircling) over the surface of the water" **(Genesis 1:2)**.

Creativity requires movement and action. God created you to move toward something. He never intended for you to remain in one place or stagnant regardless of your failures or successes.

Bible starts in a dark place (Genesis) and journeys us down Route 66 (The 66 Books of the Bible) into the marvelous destination of light (Revelation).

It's only when we stall or stop that we find ourselves headed into a form of darkness, formlessness, or captivity. This **backwards** state is usually or can be disguised as the following: death, divorce, denounced, disease, depression, deceitfulness, disdain, denial, demeaned, delay, disorder, deception, dissatisfaction, destruction, disenfranchised, disagreement, disgraced, disengagement, dismemberment or desertion. There are many other D's that are all designed to lead you into dysfunctionality or despair. But, don't you quit!!

Regardless of what we encounter, we must keep *moving forward* toward our visions and goals. Bishop Garlington, pastor of Covenant Church of Pittsburgh, said: *"The enemy wants you to see life as a still picture, but God wants you to see it as a motion picture."*

There is no greater authority bestowed upon men or women who create with the next generation in mind. They have a greater capacity for success because their thinking surpasses beyond the now. They foresee and anticipate obstacles and challenges and are able to plan around them, seeing negatives as assets of opportunity as opposed to obstructions or impossibilities.

God's mind has unlimited thoughts and His Spirit has power and boundaries that supersedes any tragedy or challenge and transforms them into victorious triumphs in every endeavor He inspires your mind to do.

Power of Prayer + Meditation + Planning = Seeing

Prayer, *meditation* and *planning* are a powerful combination. God should always be number one on your list because He is "**The First Step to seeing through faith!**" The first step of God's plan will be trans-generational. It broadens every capacity for success because you immediately take yourself out of the present day equation and include people who are not even able to contribute to the plan until further down the line. For example, at the time of this writing, I have three offspring. They are 27, 20 and 19 years of age.

These three young adults factor heavily into my life's plan. The youngest children will eventually factor into the thought processes that exist now for their eldest sibling. Just as God has planned for the future of His children and each succeeding generation, so must I...

Planning trans-generationally (more in Chapter's 2 and 3) forces me to *see* beyond today's tiny obstacles that may hinder my immediate success. However, these challenges become insignificant, even though they are real in nature. As I create strategies and identify positions for my children, they may not know that they are an important piece of the plan. Because of my children and God's mandated responsibility, I am able to overcome any minor or major *perceived* setbacks.

This way of thinking is biblical and it works. Throughout the entire Bible, the *beginning* of many stories and events were preceded by a command or vision for the present or future from God. He spoke a promise to Isaiah the prophet who wrote: The Lord of host has sworn saying:

"Surely just as I have intended so it has happened, and just as I have planned so it will stand" **(Isaiah 14:24 underline emphasis mine)**.

God has **planned** and spoken commands and promises to His prophets that have come to pass or will come to pass. He has planned and spoken a word (promise) about you, and He will be watching over that promise and you to be sure it is performed. He put His Word in you and according to the prophet Jeremiah, He is obligated to watch over it to bring it to pass the moment you tell Him, "**I see it!**" (Jeremiah 1:11). It is not because of you, but because His promise is His Word and He never lies. The instant you agree with God, He will **send** His Word to perform His promise.

He asked Jeremiah, "What do you see?" Jeremiah's response was, "I see the rod of an almond tree!" Then the Lord said to Jeremiah, "You have seen well, for I am watching over My Word to perform it" (Jeremiah 1:12). The apostle Paul adds credence to God's promises. He describes God's promise to Abraham in his letter to the Romans when He wrote:

In hope against hope he believed, so that he might become a father of many nations according to that which had been spoken "SO, SHALL YOUR DESCENDANTS BE." Without becoming weak in faith he contemplated his own body, now as good as dead since he was about one hundred years old, and the deadness of Sarah's womb; yet, with respect to the promise of God, he did not waiver in unbelief but grew strong in faith, giving glory to God, and being fully assured that what God had promised, He was able to perform **(Romans 4:18-21)**.

He said, "Descendants" (children, offspring, and young) not ascendants. God blesses downward to the next generation. We have become a selfish generation that is stuck on and in ourselves and have not considered the trans-generational concept in which God mandates to establish His kingdom from generation to generation. Even at 100 years of age Abraham, *"grew strong"* in faith because of the promise. Again, He stated, "Because of the Promise!" Moreover, he made it a point to build an altar for God at certain junctures of his journey. He would use these altars to pray, to seek direction, and to bless God as he was blessed.

Moses wrote:

"The Lord appeared to Abram and said, "To your descendants I will give you this land. So, he built an altar there to the Lord who had appeared to him" (Genesis 12: 6-7).

You must confer through prayer with God to **see** what plans He has said for your life, purpose, and destiny. Again, God said:

"I am watching over My word to perform it" (Jeremiah 1:12).

I must translate this Scripture one more time for you! When you have agreed with GOD about His word inside of you, He will be WATCHING OVER YOU! Because His Word is inside of you and through your faith, trust, and works, "It" has to come to pass...

We should *pursue* with extreme diligence in prayer to **see** a WORD *(promise)* from God, and by Faith, to live and work with the expectation of Him watching over (Security and Protection) the spoken Word and you to guarantee its performance. In many instances we are not taught to search after God and His promise for our lives. Instead, we think it will just drop out of the sky. The closer you get to God, who is the Originator of all creation, the more creative you will become with new ideas.

Note: God does not do repeat performances, man does!

Roberta Flack and the late, Donny Hathaway sang a beautiful song called, "The Closer I Get to You, the More You Make Me See." God is saying to you, "The *Closer* You Get to *Me* the More I let You See" (Paraphrased). Prayer is the journey to intimacy with God. I said 'journey' because He has so much for us to *see* that our sight has to be spiritually adjusted to observe all the gradual impartation's of His vision for our lives.

As He gives us time to mature, our prayer lives must reflect regular sessions of intimate encounters of spirit and truth. He has to remove the scales from our eyes, condition our hearts, and cleanse us from sin to receive His Spirit in order for us truly to do His will.

In the Book of Ezekiel, God said:

Then I will sprinkle clean water on you, and you will be clean; I will cleanse you from all your filthiness and from your idols. Moreover, I will give you a new heart and put a new spirit within you and cause you to walk in My statues, and you will be careful to observe My ordinance (Ezekiel 36:25-27).

One of the most disappointing experiences in my life was to finally get a reasonable amount of money or security and still feel empty. The myth that money and fame will give you peace and joy is an age-old tale. We have all read about celebrities or famous people whom express their emptiness and struggles or have seen the sad and tragic ending of an unfulfilled life.

They envisioned a life of fulfillment, but after reaching a certain plateau they often felt dejected, lost, and empty. They were seeking to fill the void that only God can. The need for God is the same whether people are poor or rich. We all came directly from God. There is an inherited-spiritual-magnetism that naturally draws us back to the Source of our existence.

God is Sovereign

We must never detach ourselves from the Origin of our creation. Just as water returns to its natural place of distribution, we do the same. Job's experience was one of few that gave no logical explanation to common thought at the time of his affliction. After a series of major losses and tragic occurrences he chose to continue to believe and trust in God. The general thought of the day was surely he had done something very wrong. Regardless of the amount of affliction Job encountered, he refused to dishonor God. Instead, he proclaimed:

"Naked I came from my mother's womb, and naked I shall return there. The Lord gave and the Lord has taken away. Blessed be the name of the Lord" **(Job 1:21).**

Job could speak from his experience. He lost his children, fortune, health, influence, and most of his friends. He was certainly qualified to instruct us with the truth of God's sovereignty. However, he remained faithful, said:

"Submit to God, and you will have peace; then things will go well for you. Listen to His instructions, and store them in your heart. If you return to the Almighty, you will be restored-so clean up your life. If you give up your lust for money and throw your precious gold into the river, the Almighty himself will be your treasure. He will be your precious silver! Then you take delight in the Almighty and look up to God. You will pray to Him, and He will hear you, and you will fulfill your vows to Him. You will succeed in whatever you choose to do, and light will shine on the road ahead of you. If people are in trouble and you say, 'help them,' God will save them. Even sinners will be rescued; they will be rescued because your hands are pure" **(Job 22:21-30).**

The apostle Peter wrote: *"Therefore humble yourselves under the mighty hand of God, that He may exalt you at the proper time"* **(1 Peter 5:6).**

I encourage you to read Job's story in its entirety. Midway through a plethora of perils, Job repented and began **seeing** God again. Even though he never actually condemned God, he realized that his attitude and countenance at times was sometimes unpleasant.

Lastly, Job stopped **his** complaining, murmuring, humbled himself; and acknowledged the Almighty and Sovereign God. Because of his change of attitude and **view** of God, God restored his health, and gave him a new family, grandchildren, new possessions; plus much more. Actually, He gave him **double** for his **trouble**.

It takes total trust in God to surrender your desires and believe by faith in what He reveals to you through revelation and His Word. He will always validate His vision for us with signs, wonders, and His Word. As we pray, our hearts are filled with His spirit. We will begin to **see** with greater clarity and understanding of what His purpose is for our lives.

In addition, we become instruments of righteousness in His heavenly symphony as we are directed to play tunes which praise His **holy performances**. What a marvelous experience to have the ability to start a new life anytime one desires, with creations divinely orchestrated by the Master of All creation!

There is no greater planner man can ever seek than the Master Planner of this universe! As you begin a consistent life of prayer and meditative planning in God you will be able to *see* the very creative tributaries within Him begin to flow into you, saturating your every thought, emotion, and imagination to propel you to *see* things you have never *seen*.

It is God's way of revealing new beginnings to individuals devoted to prayer. He has so much for those willing to discard their plans and trust in Him as He prepares to journey us down the road to glory for an experience beyond our wildest dreams. Our God *never disappoints* when He *appoints*.

The apostle Paul wrote:

That is what the Scriptures mean when they say, "No eye has seen, no ear has heard, and no mind has imagined what God has for those who love Him." But it was to us that God revealed these things by his Spirit for the Spirit searches out everything and shows us God's deep secrets. No one can know a person's thoughts except that person's own spirit and no one can know God's thoughts except God's own Spirit. And we have received God's Spirit (not the world's spirit), so we can know the wonderful things God has freely given us" **(1 Corinthians 2:9-12, NLT)**.

Prayer and meditation opens our spiritual eyes to *see* God in a capacity beyond our carnal perception. He asked Jeremiah, "What do you see?" The word *see* means: to perceive by the eye; to perceive or detect as if by sight: to have experience of; to come to know; to form a mental picture of; to perceive the meaning or import; to be aware of: to imagine as a possibility. This question to the prophet was to be answered with a spiritual response, not an earthly one. God's interrogation of Jeremiah was to induce him into seeing the spiritual evidence of His Word based on His promise!

Lastly, I have extracted from the Bible a few more of His many prophesies and promises spoken to you from His prophets. Read and meditate on what God says about His Word. God is forward moving and forever calling (encouraging) us to change. He is the only *Past, Now and Future God!*

You may wish to make these verses a part of your daily Bible readings. When possible, read them aloud for greater spiritual impact and fortification.

1. *"I am the Lord, that is My name; I will not give My glory to another, Nor My praise to graven images. "Behold, the former things have come to pass, Now I declare new things; before they spring forth I proclaim them to you"* (Isaiah 42:8-9).

2. *"Thus says the Lord who made the earth, the Lord who formed it to establish it, the Lord His name, 'Call to me and I will answer and tell you great and mighty things, which you do not know"* (Jeremiah 33:3).

3. *"For I know the plans I have for you,"* declares the LORD, *"plans to prosper you and not to harm you, plans to give you hope and a future"* (Jeremiah 29:11).

4. *The word of the Lord came to me saying "What do you see, Jeremiah?" And I said; "I see the rod of an almond tree." Then the Lord said to me, You have seen well, for I am watching over my word to perform it"* (Jeremiah 1:11-12).

5. *Then the Lord Said unto me, "Son of man, stand on your feet that I may speak with you!" As He spoke to me the Spirit entered me and set me on my feet; And I heard Him speaking to me* (Ezekiel 2:1-2).

6. *Then Lord answered me and said, "Write the vision and make it plain upon tables, that he may run that readeth it"* **(Habakkuk 2:2)**.

7. *Now all this took place to fulfill what was spoken by the Lord through the prophets: "Behold, THE VIRGIN SHALL BE WITH CHILD AND SHALL BARE A SON, AND THEY SHALL CALL HIS NAME IMMANUEL," which translated means, "GOD BE WITH US"* **(Matthew 1:22-23)**.

8. *But He answered and said: "IT IS WRITTEN, 'MAN SHALL NOT LIVE ON BREAD ALONE, BUT ON EVERY WORD THAT PROCEED OUT OF THE MOUTH OF GOD"* **(Matthew 4:4)**.

9. *And Jesus said unto them, "Follow Me, and I will make you become fishers of men"* **(Mark 1:17)**.

10. *But He answered and said to them, "My mother and My brother are these who hear the word of God and do it"* **(Luke 8:21)**.

11. *So Jesus said to them, "My time is not yet here, but your time is always opportune"* **(John 7:6)**.

12. *"Behold, I am coming quickly, and My reward is with me, to render to every man according to what he has done. "I am the Alpha and the Omega, the first and the last, the beginning and the end"* **(Revelation 22:12-13)**.

Chapter Two
Call to God: What are You Saying to Me Now?

We are experiencing the most challenging era of change in every corner of the world. People every where seem exhausted, frustrated, and at the brink of despair. Our nations are in a perilous state of hopelessness. The call for democracy is failing, and no one appears to have answers to the mounting problems that are permeating and plaguing whole nations. The citizens of autocratic governments are calling for an end to dictatorships.

They are rising up and demanding freedom, liberty and transformation. These nations have been ruled by one man and his hand-picked governments that have denied them of basic liberties of life and have repressed their creativity. More than ever, we all need to stop, call, and listen to what God is saying to us now!

People born into repressed nations are now calling for these dictators who do not allow their dreams, visions or ideas to flourish to be banished from their rule by other free-nations, or they are overthrowing these dictators by force. Imagine living in a world where your goals and dreams mean nothing, and you have no rights or freedom to express your God given gifts, visions, and aspirations when you are forced to acknowledge a man as a self-proclaim supreme being, who wants his citizens to call on him for their visions.

A dictator's goal is to live opulently from the efforts, labor and sweat of their controlled, intimidated and demoralized citizens. They rule by force and threats of imprisonment or even death. We, who are fortunate enough to live in nations that allow us to pray, create and exercise our faith, take this marvelous privilege for granted by often wasting years of valuable productivity because we do not purpose to call on God for divine revelations.

God has made creativity an open invitation for all who seek to venture into the unknowns of His great and mighty works. With simplicity, He repeats His principles for creativity in various books in the Bible. He sits in heaven and practically compels you and me to call on Him for ideas and visions of creativity. However, we neglect His golden opportunities of relevance. What God will reveal to us in our intimate time in prayer will always be cutting edge and progressive.

Today, I, as well as the Holy Spirit, want you to prove God. Call on Him and see how He will reveal things you have never seen, and through your faith and works you will become creators of mighty and wonderful works you could never imagine. So, I dare you, yes you, to take this moment and incorporate a strategic plan to dedicate to prayer, meditation and calling on God for exciting possibilities that will give you purpose and passion in every area of your life.

First, for clarity, allow me to define what the word **_call_** means: request, noise, cry, plea, demand, song and appeal... You can use some of these words to state your case to God. Please do!

Remember what He told Jeremiah?:

"Thus says the Lord who made the earth, the Lord who formed it to establish it, the Lord is His name, 'Call to me and I will answer and tell you great and mighty things, which you do not know"
(Jeremiah 33:3).

Today, I challenge you to create now! What is God saying to you? ***Call to Me and I will answer and tell you great and know."*** Today is your first step to a new beginning! As you call to God, He **will** answer and begin His divine impartation of revelations for your life.

We are Nations without a Vision

In most nations there are not enough jobs and industries to fill the growing demand for gainful employment. A nation cannot thrive and grow without a vision or an industrial and manufacturing base. China is one of few nations truly growing because they are producing goods and we are buying and distributing their products among ourselves. America has become a nation of borrowers, information traders, consumers, and distributors with not much vision for the future in *industrialization* and *manufacturing*.

We are trading information and not products. It is comparable to Junk Bonds (also known as a high-yield bonds or speculative bonds). These bonds are high risk transactions with most of them having questionable value, but they come with the high hopes of lucrative returns. We must begin to produce tangible products that come out of the earth from natural resources and from our own country. No nation can continue to consume goods from other countries and not produce comparable products to export. We are investing in other countries because we see little vision for America. 27

It is impossible to balance such a disparity of imported goods and America is not producing equal or greater goods to be sold inside or outside of our borders.

This concept negates basic economics principles, and if we maintain this trend, we will have to continue borrowing money from the very nations exploiting us with over-importation of cheaply made products. China has a vision for their nation. They are lending America money to subsidize our economy, which is in direct violation of God's principles. He commanded that we do not borrow, but lend. Saying:

"For the LORD your God will bless you as He has promised you, and you will lend to many nations, but you will not borrow; and you will rule over many nations, but they will not rule over you" (Deuteronomy 15:6).

The Bible clearly states: *"Just as the rich rule the poor, so the borrower is servant to the lender"* (Proverbs 22:7).

When we become dependent upon other countries or persons to finance our future, they will eventually control and dictate their agenda for our lives. The act of financial disobedience gives the lender direct access to the security and legacy of our nation and homes. America must become fiscally responsible as a nation, and our leaders must recognize the imminent danger of our nation becoming an open smörgåsbord for China to serve any dish they desire to us because their money gives them the power to do so.

The fact that we have hundreds of vacant factories and millions of square feet of empty warehouse space in every major city in America is indicative of us having become a nation of borrowers, consumers, and distributors. In 2005, a reporter stated, "I spoke with President Clinton on the eve of the *Clinton Global Initiative's* annual meeting in New York Monday, where "jobs, jobs, jobs" is one of the main topics of the conference. Former President Bill Clinton says, "The American Dream has been under assault for 30 years" (Aaron Task).

We must begin manufacturing and producing goods and services in America again in order to turn our economy around. I have customers who sit in their offices all day trading and answering emails for days on end. When there are no tangible products or services associated with these massive exchanges of messages and information those jobs will eventually disappear. We must have sustaining labor or products to support the workers income.

This problem has been the demise of middle management in corporate America and around the world. Hear the truth! God drives the economies of the world. It is He that sends ideas and witty inventions to man to make and create jobs. Our nation is prostituting the future of our children and our children's, children and possibly national security for unprecedented corporate profitability with the exportation of gainful employment to other nations that don't believe in God, His Son, or our countries philosophies.

For the first time in recent history, we have run out of ideas to stimulate the economy. Entire nations, including America, would be in dire straits if our governments did not print new (more in Chapter 10) money to infuse their economies; they would have collapsed. God was very specific in the Book of Deuteronomy when He stated rather sternly:

"But you shall remember the Lord your God, for it is He who is giving you power to make wealth that He may confirm His covenant which He swore to your fathers, as it is this day. It shall come about if you ever forget the Lord, your God and go after other gods and serve them and

worship them, I testify against you today you will surely perish. Like the nations that the Lords makes to perish before you, so you shall perish; because you would not listen to the voice of the Lord your God" **(Deuteronomy 8:18-20)**.

America's power and wealth came from God to establish His kingdom. We have established vile, decrepit, and desolate cities full of crime, lawlessness, and idols. Only God can fix this mess! As we turn our hearts back to Him, He will FORGIVE US and give us creative visions, ideas, and directions. The farther we get from the source (God), the less creative we become. The more creative we get, the closer we are to God. Man will not resolve our problems without God, nor will America and other nations prosper. Our forefathers weaved God into the very fiber of our government, but our new *fathers* and **mothers** are cutting Him out.

Our Founding Fathers referred to God as the "Supreme Judge"—a reference taken from the Holy Bible, our Christian Constitution and included it in the "Declaration of Independence." This international problem will affect every citizen eventually. History only repeats itself. China is projected to be the world's economic and military power in the foreseeable future because America and the other previously powerful Christian nations refused to obey God's laws and fell from His grace.

Unfortunately, unless America repents and honors God, China will rise above us. If China does surpass America and not honor God and His statues, it will only follow us in the same demise. We must pray that every nation return to God, and we must start with our leaders. In his first major foreign policy address in Charleston, SC., GOP (Republican Party) 2012 presidential candidate Mitt Romney stated:

"This century must be an American century. In an American century, America has the strongest economy and the strongest military in the world," Romney says. "God did not create this country to be a nation of followers. America is not destined to be one of several equally balanced global powers. America must lead the world, or someone else will."

I stated previously that regardless of where you find yourself, God has a divine plan and purpose for our nation and your life. At any time or any place, all we have to do is pray. It is that simple. God clearly said:

"For I know the plans that I have for you," declares the Lord, 'plans for welfare and not for calamity to give you a future and a hope. 'Then you will call upon Me and come and pray to Me and I will listen to you. You will seek Me and fine Me when you search for Me with all your heart. I will be found by you,' declares the Lord, 'and I will restore your fortunes and will gather you from the nations and from all the places where I have driven you.' declares the Lord, and I will bring you back to the place from where I sent you into exile' **(Jeremiah 29:11-14)**.

The majority of us are not pleasing God. Even if you have a decent career, home, money in the bank, and a loving relationship, have you truly asked God, "Is this the plan that You have for me?"

More than likely, you haven't. I remember when my Telecom Business was a success and growing, I was assured this was my life's vocation. I later discovered that it never was. I had never taken the time to confer in prayer with God for what He desired for me. I believe many others feel the same.

Today, I hope you will be honest with yourself and assess your current state of being. God said, "He drove us out of our lands (nations) because of our sins and brought us into exile and separated us as well." The definition of Nation is: State, country, land, realm, homeland, people, population and inhabitants.

He will send other nations to take our land or send us into some form of exile. I must also give the meanings of (exile) as defined: banished, deport, sent away, expel, cast out and separate. I referenced these meanings to help you understand that it is God who allows a nation to fall, because we leave Him and disobey His word, what He has for us. Just as Adam and Eve were banished from the Garden of Eden because of their sin, so will we be. However, God loves us so much that He eagerly waits for us to repent and turn toward Him for the plans He has for our lives, as He stated to Jeremiah:

"Seek Me and I shall be found by you when you search for me with all of you heart" (Jeremiah 29:13).

Call God for Your Vision or Man for His Provisions

Now, before you go any further, I challenge you; yes **YOU** to read the prophet Habakkuk's statement:

"I will stand upon my watch, and set me upon the tower, and will watch to see what He will say unto me, and what I shall answer when I am reproved. And the Lord answered me and said, "Write the vision, and make it plain upon tables, that he may run that read it. For the vision is yet for an appointed time, but at the end it shall speak, and not lie; because it will surely come, it will not tarry" (Habakkuk 2:1-3).

I will repeat his first statement. He stated, "And the Lord answered me and said, **Write** the vision and make it plain." **How simple does it get?** God answered Habakkuk because he called on Him. He was being reproved by God! Obviously, he was rebuked and reprimanded for his disobedience. How long was he going to stand at the watch, waiting and not writing?

If God was reproving Habakkuk, it's because He had already shown him the vision before, but Habakkuk did not write it upon tables the first time.

I promise you this: if you call on God, He will answer you in His perfect time and give you His vision for your life when you call on Him. Truthfully, there are only two life styles: (1) A life of visions from God. (2) A life of provisions from man. These are distinct and true!! Allow me to expound in reality. A life of **visions** are _God-inspired_, and has no limits and is infinite in its capacity to create and provide continuously. A life of **provisions** are **man-controlled** and is only limited and regulated by man's ability to provide, control, and dictate temporarily his or hers agenda for your life

Depending on a man or woman is totally contrary to what God created us to be. It is clearly written in the Book of Genesis:

"God blessed them; and said to them, "Be fruitful and multiply, and fill the earth, and subdue it; and rule over the fish of the sea and birds of the sky and over every living thing that moves on the earth"
(Genesis 1:28).

The majority of people in our world (except for those in Autocratic Nations) are waiting to be told the directions for their lives. Ironically, the only thing that separates the successful from the unsuccessful is calling on **God—faith, vision, planning and works (action), period!**

In the Book Genesis, there's a classic example of two brothers with a vision from God. They both knew the destiny for their lives. However, the younger brother knew the importance and concept of trans-generational living while the older brother forfeited his legacy for the temporary satisfaction of man's provision. It is detailed in this story written by Moses in _firstborn_ (Genesis 25:27-34).

As the Boys grew up, Esau became a skillful hunter. He was an outdoorsman, but Jacob had a quiet temperament, preferring to stay home. Isaac loved Esau because He enjoyed eating the wild game Esau brought home, but Rebecca loved Jacob. One day when Jacob was cooking some stew, Esau arrived from the wilderness exhausted and hungry. Esau said to Jacob, "I'm starved! Give me some of that stew!" (This is how Esau got his other name, Edom, which means "red.") All right Jacob replied, "But trade me your rights as firstborn son." "Look, I'm dying of starvation! What good is my birthright to me now?" But Jacob said, "First you must swear that your birthright is mine."

So Esau swore an oath, thereby selling all his rights as the firstborn to his brother, Jacob. Then Jacob gave Esau some bread and lentil stew. Esau ate the meal, then got up and left. He showed contempt for his rights as the firstborn (**Message Bible**).

This story illustrates what happens if you don't take God's visions for your life seriously, how you will vicariously forfeit your birthright to success. A birthright gives possession, privilege, and rights that are one's due by birth or a special privilege afforded a first-born. It is our inalienable birthright as sons and daughters of God to prosper. When we repeatedly exchange our future and the futures of the generations that follow for a measly man-provided handout, we satisfy only our immediate requirements and continue down the same path of discontent, despair, and disillusionment.

God will use man to provide for us temporarily, but His original plan is that we become dependent upon Him as the source of creativity, vision, and provisions. God is not pleased when we constantly **call on man** for our visions or provisions. He calls those who repeat such behavior a godless and immoral person. The unknown writer expressed this rather plainly, saying:

*"That **there** be no immoral or godless person like Esau, who sold his own birthright for a single meal. For you know that even afterwards, when he desired to inherit the blessing, he was rejected, for he found no place for repentance, though he **sought** for it with tears"* **(Hebrews 12:16-17, bold emphasis mine).**

More importantly, why would I continue to call on man for his provisions for my life when I can call on God for His visions, my future, and the futures of generations that follow me? Again, man can only provide for my immediate needs and dictate the use of my creativity. God, however, will give me visions to create a future of unlimited opportunities and possibilities, and the liberty to expand it beyond the provisions of man's limited capacity. I based this fact solely upon man's human inability to only provide, temporary and externally to the condition of his heart.

Habakkuk 2: 1 means: Call on God for the vision for your life, and when He answers, get a pencil, paper, write it down, make it plain, simple, detailed, precise, work, and wait. You will never figure out how God operates or what schedule He's on.

Reminder: He will never be on your timetable!

In the Book of Mark:

Jesus explains to the disciples how God plans. He said, "But on that day or hour no one knows, not even the angels in heaven, nor the Son, but the Father alone. "Take heed, keep on the alert; for you do not know when the appointed time will come" **(Mark 13:32-33).**

Notice what He said, "For you do not know when the appointed time will come." God is telling you, "Wait, for it will surely come" and at the end "it shall speak and not lie" (Emphases mine); meaning in order to have an "end" you must have a beginning! So, again, I say to you, call on God, write the vision and make it plain.

Allow me to explain what *waiting* is as defined by my dictionary: in the making, for the future, to come, before you, ahead of you and coming up.

Lastly, my definition of *waiting*: is: as a waiter serves at a restaurant. You must begin waiting and serving the Lord and His people as a waiter does... It would be a great opportunity for you to serve and to be *mentored* in the arena of your vision. Jesus Himself expressed this to His disciples how He was mentored by His Father in the epistle of John:

So Jesus explained himself at length. "I'm telling you this straight. The Son can't independently do a thing, only what He sees the Father doing. What the Father does, the Son does. The Father loves the Son and includes Him in everything He is doing." **(John 5:19, Message Bible)**.

There are countless stories of people who waited (served) on people in their industries, vocations, and work before their vision was realized. God is a true servant leader, He commands us to pass on what we have learned to the next generation.

The late, Dr. Myles Munroe, pastor and author, stated:

"If we do not mentor, we create chaos. A good example of weak mentoring is Solomon, who did not groom anyone to follow him. David mentored Solomon, but after Solomon died the Kingdom was divided and destroyed."—Passing It On

The Bible gives numerous examples of mentoring partnerships: God and Abraham, Moses and Joshua, David and Solomon, Naomi and Ruth, Elijah and Elisha, Mordecai and Esther, Pharaoh and Joseph, Elizabeth and Mary, God and Jesus and His disciples and Paul and Timothy.

In other words you must find a godly mentor and wait (serve) on him or her.

Truth: You must have a mentor!

A mentor will expose you to an environment to *show* you how to accomplish your vision and make it plain. In Dr. Myles Munroe's book, "Passing It On," he also wrote:

"Moses was authentic. He was secure in his position—Just as Joshua was secure in his. He was a servant, the aid—in other words, the one who was there to do anything and everything the leader needs. In fact, an aide out thinks you, always watches to see what you are thinking of doing next and does it for you."

Emphasis: You will never experience any major degree of success without an earthly mentor. He or she will coach and prevent you from encountering unnecessary pitfalls and anguish as you tarry towards the vision for your life. However, God wants us to call on Him for revelation, and He uses relationships as a way to prepare us for t h e journey He has for us. Faith requires that we charter unknown waters often, but God never leaves us without a person and a path for success.

Therefore, I encourage you to call on God, write the vision, make it plain and He will show you great and mighty things that only He can decree, while you are waiting and serving those who are in your life to mentor, coach and lead you through the plans God has for your life.

Today, now, you can visualize in prayer the plan God desires for you to live and begin creating your life by faith, works (action) and by the will of God! He says:

"Delight yourself in the Lord; And He will give you the desires of your heart. Commit your way to the Lord, Trust also in Him, and He will do it" **(Psalm 37:4-5)**.

God's plans for our lives are far greater than what we could ever imagine. If we can trust Him and do what He presents to us in prayer, we will never be disappointed. He says, *"Trust in the Lord with all of your heart and lean not on your own understanding"* **(Proverbs 3:5)**.

Jesus **expressed** this promise to a desperate father in need of healing for his son: And Jesus said unto him:

"All things are possible to him who believes.' Immediately the boy's father cried out and said, I do believe; help my unbelief" **(Mark 9:23-24)**.

The apostle Mark was rather unique in his Gospel. He emphasized urgency with the word "IMMEDIATELY" in his writings. My dictionary defines immediately as right way, straightaway, at once, directly, without delay, instantaneously. These terms are all synonymous with 'Now.' You can create a life of absolute opulence, grandeur, beauty, prosperity, health, power, love, peace, joy, and so forth, but it all begins with *prayer, faith, vision, planning, and action.* However, you must do it, *now* and *immediately.*

When God Answers: You Must Plan

King Solomon was a great advisor of planning. He wrote:

"Commit your works to the Lord and your plans will be established. The Lord has made everything for its own purpose, even the wicked for the day of evil" **(Proverbs 16:3-4)**.

As the saying goes, "If you fail to plan, you are planning to fail!" There is also another saying that should impel you to plan: "If you don't know where you are going, any road will get you there" (James Galimore).

In life, you are either leading, following, or stuck (idle or dying); there is no in between. Planning sets in motion order, thought and reason.

Planning forces you to structure discipline and strategies when the appointed windows of opportunity open and helps you to navigate through the unforeseen challenges, pitfalls, and changes. We should always live in the mental mode of expectation; it keeps us from drifting in and out of the past and moving forward.

Important Truth: You cannot plan for the PAST!!

Planning is comparable to preparing for a short or long term vacation. Its unique purpose is essentially to design the venture around your arrival, your stay, and your departure. Planning gives you a broader perspective of what the vision entails and the most logical way to get there.

Planning ignites and incites creativity beyond measure and allows you to see the future as its being unveiled before the very presence of the planner. It presents a preview of all the possibilities and paints a portrait powerful enough to inspire and motivate action and participation to all who read it.

When writing your plan, it is essential that you keep it plain and concise. You should be able to express it with precision and clarity in order to avoid confusion and misunderstanding. At the point of presentation, it should flow with relative simplicity; detailing points of strategy, purpose, and benefit. Moreover, it must be done with consciousness of time and projected collaboration. I have been in corporate meetings where we would haggle around and around, discussing how to accomplish a certain plan with the least amount of difficulties and cost.

What I discovered most often was that the longer the meetings, the more chaos and confusion, usually resulting in major time and money being wasted. Unfortunately, time is the only invaluable resource that you cannot recapture. You must determine never to allow anyone to squander this precious commodity. Successful people will *never* allow you to waste their time!

Your life: It is not a dress rehearsal. Each of us has the same amount time in a day (24-hours) to prepare, plan, and implement our goals. I promise you this, if you do not know what to do with your time some successful, unsuccessful or talent savvy person will recognize your gifts and use them for their gain. If they see that you respect and value you and your time, then they will respect and value you too. You must know where you are going and what you are doing at all times.

I will give you some great practical life changing advice, which I beseech you, to never forget. Your life is a story. You are either at the ***beginning,*** in the ***middle*** or toward the ***ending***. In a story, there are six concepts that must be applied, and these same concepts are relevant in each of our lives!

The Six Concepts of Life

If you apply these concepts when planning your short, medium or long range goals, you will rarely, if ever, miss the *target*. The six concepts of your life's story are, ***Who***, ***What***, ***Where***, ***When***, ***Why***, and ***How***. These concepts are typical of any book, play, or movie in any arena in the world. Your life is a reality show, not some science-fiction story or some imaginative performance that started with a blur. You will live these concepts or they will live you!!

They are interwoven into our lives whether we're cognizant of them or not. They have played a vital role in shaping our past and will play an equally vital role in determining our future. However, today, you will begin to control and plan your destiny using these concepts. If you grasp these concepts and apply them daily into your planning and future activities, you will be literally **writing** the novel or living in the *motion* picture of success for your life.

Let me repeat that: If you grasp these concepts and apply them daily into your planning and future activities you will be literally **writing** the novel or living in the *motion* picture of success for your life. I will give you a condensed explanation of each concept. However, please elaborate on them further as you begin your planning process.

Who, What, Where, When, Why, and How!

1. **WHO** tells me whom to include or whom to avoid. The importance of choosing the right supporting cast is absolutely paramount, for these individuals can't be in opposition or competition with your goals. They must be value adders and encouragers. They must see the vision and play a cooperative and beneficially compensational role in seeing the vision come to fruition. Any person with a negative or discouraging attitude must be excluded and dismissed.

2. **WHAT** defines the GOAL and target of intent and must be articulated clearly to the casting members with enthusiasm and clarity. Each member must know his or her roles as defined and agreed upon in carrying out the task. All must be willing to stay on one accord at each stage of progress. Failure to maintain harmony will abort the plan or disrupt the flow of success. Lastly, as the leader, you must keep

everyone apprised of the state of the vision and what it takes to stay focused in accomplishing the goal.

3. **WHERE** denotes the geographical territory needed to build or create with future growth. This concept requires a demographical strategy and ongoing surveys of a specific region for potential opportunity, progress, and prosperity. Careful studies and statistical data must be acquired and analyzed. Also, exploration of income, people, and resources. This process will require an ongoing effort of keeping this information current and forwardmoving.

4. **WHEN** is the appointed time of launching the vision? After all of the careful planning, team members are equipped and trained, the puzzle has all of the pieces together, and the picture is ready for hanging. The members are all on one accord and the success is inevitable. Weekly to frequent meetings to monitor and alter plans if necessary are a must. Constant communication from all the team members is pertinent to the progress of meeting the weekly goals.

5. **WHY** gives the logistics and reasoning behind purpose and strategies to accomplish goals. Knowing why is the key that drives the vision in the right direction. Each facet of the plan must be followed and complied with in order for each component to interconnect for the overall vision to come tofruition. Occasionally, this concept as well as the others might require a gradual shift from the original plan but will not drastically unless some unforeseen major challenge occurs. If solid it will remain, regardless of the changes of plans, and continue usually for days, weeks, months or possibly years.

6. **HOW** encapsulates all of the other five concepts and evaluates the purpose for each person, place, or thing needed to reach the desired (goal) target. This concept is a very simple, yet profound, self- applied strategy that actually works.

If you apply these concepts, you will rarely, if ever, venture into futile and meaningless efforts. In my 30 years of business experiences, I have deduced that the two common denominators amongst the wealthy and successful are planning and time management. The other two common denominators among the poor and unsuccessful are lack of planning and neglect to manage and respect time. A wealthy friend of mine once said: *"Most people that have money don't waste time, but most people that waste time don't have money."*

These six basic concepts practiced and applied in your personal and business life, coupled with strategic planning, will inevitably lead you to success and, in most cases, prosperity!

Choosing Your Government

I have provided a format that will require you to recruit two people per concept for a total of twelve (your government) to help you accomplish your goals. Again, neglecting to *pray* for your selections will guarantee you delays, disappointment, or possible destruction. The biblical number for twelve (12) represents: government, foundation, and completion. The word government means: to administrate, to manage, to control, to direct, to regiment, to rule, to supervise, and to command. These attributes must correlate with the twelve because you cannot live a good life of success without governing and being governed. I use *to* for emphasis only...

Fact: A nation cannot operate successfully without a body (government) of people participating in the vision and goals of that nation. When a government is without laws, statues, and principles and order is not applied, that country falls into chaos, loss of liberty, and often death to its citizens. The same is true in our lives!! The twelve people you choose will help govern you and keep you accountable and moving forward in the vision God has for your life.

Jesus used this concept with His twelve disciples and became very successful in His earthly ministry. You must not regard this practice as obsolete or archaic it is a proven principle that works. You must choose twelve people as your government to fill the six concepts of your life's plan. They must have experience in the areas you are endeavoring to pursue.

Your plans may or will require you to cultivate new, meaningful, mutually-beneficial-relationships with wise people who have been where you are going or have proven experience in areas of logistics, organization, networking, administration, finances and other skill sets needed for your advancement.

Important Truth: No <u>man</u> or <u>woman</u> is an island!

If you function alone you will never reach your God given destiny. He created us to be interdependent on others. They do not have to be Christians, but should be strong in character, morals, and integrity. Optimistically, they will be converted by the Christian example of love demonstrated by you and your government. Jesus and His twelve disciples proved to the world that this concept works; however, it's rarely used by Christians! I believe these six concepts will add value and foundation to the plans and future of your life.

Truth: You cannot advance your plans without your government!

This concept should be used and practiced throughout your life, for it will keep you moving, changing, and innovative. You will not always use the same twelve, but as your life plans change or are accomplished, you will be refreshed with new people, new ideas, and new influences. You must always keep twelve people as your core group of foundation because they represent the systems, networks, relationships, and *government* you will need for life (More in Chapter 6).

Allow me to share with you an example in the Scriptures of how important choosing the right *government* is and giving them a title to identify with their purposes and responsibilities. Jesus was serious about His government of disciples; He did not choose any of them without conferring (praying) with God first.

Luke gives a vivid description in his Gospel when he wrote:

It was at this time that He went off to the mountain to pray, and He spent the whole night in prayer to God. And when day came, He called His disciples to Him and chose twelve of them, whom He also named Apostles. Simon, whom He also named Peter, and Andrew his brother; James and John; and Philip and Bartholomew; and Matthew and Thomas; James the Son of Alphaeus, and Simon who was called the Zealot; Judas the son of James and Judas Iscariot who became a traitor **(Luke 6:12-16).**

The Bible states, "He chose twelve of them." Note: There were many others there, but Jesus selected only the twelve God revealed to Him in prayer. You should never choose people in any of your endeavors without prayer and careful consideration of the character, integrity, moral and godly standards they demonstrate. Names and titles are essential in encouragement and motivation.

They give authority and identity to the persons who are commissioned and appropriated to carry out the given task. If possible, always designate a title to each member when planning and formulating your vision. You m u s t keep each member accountable and receptive to the description of duties, authority, and responsibility they are assigned to complete. Be mindful in choosing different genders and blend like-minded personalities. They should be able to flow harmoniously within the groups.

Who (Two People) _____

_____

What (Two People) _____

_____

Where (Two People) _____

_____

When (Two People) _____

_____

Why (Two People) _____

_____

How (Two People) _____

_____

Remember: Relationships and friendships are the key to all success. They must possess knowledge and skills in areas in which you are weak. They should be strong in those areas in order to advance the vision. Keep in mind you will not advance to the next stage with people on the same level as yourself. Secondly, these twelve people will elevate your thinking and influence and expose you to new insight, ideas and associations, thereby, inviting you into a new world and new prospective.

Factored: You will never progress in a particular field without developing new relationships and friendships with people who are in the arena you are pursuing. They expose and introduce you to the people who have already accomplished your vision and most likely might be willing to help you with yours.

They also encourage you to grow and broaden your capacity to communicate and succeed in these new areas of opportunity.

You may not have all twelve (your government) people at this moment, but as you stay in prayer, focus, and strategically move towards the vision, you will meet each member of your team with the skills and wisdom you need to accomplish your vision as you get closer to your goal, it never fails.

I have personally experienced this phenomenon in my own life. I have always met people when I exposed myself to the environment in which I am purposing to endeavor.

The success of our lives and plans hinges on our ability to cultivate mutually-beneficial-relationships and friendships. There is no way to escape this basic fundamental principle for trans-generational success.

Truth #1: No Friends, No Success! No Relationships, No Success!

Truth #2: Know Friends, Know Success! Know Relationships, Know Success!

Jesus expressed this so eloquently to His disciples when He said:

"I no longer call you servants, because a servant does not know his master's business. Instead, I have called you friends, for everything that I learned from my Father I have made known to you" **(John 15:15).**

True friendships will move you into relationships and expose you to people, places, and opportunities that you could never participate in without being trustworthy, loyal, humble, diligent, and most of all honest.

Chapter Three
Writing it Decrees Your Faith

The story of God's house (Temple) being rebuilt in Jerusalem should add credence to God's command to write down His vision. There is a supernatural phenomenon that cannot be explained. When God tells you to write the vision, it is His decree or declaration that consummates the success of it and places the obligation on Him to work out the unforeseen particulars and desired outcome with your inclusions (works).

This concept-rich biblical story supersedes time lines and details the in-depth facts that you must read to grasp the divine principles of writing the vision... Please do not scan over these historical events in this beautiful story that documents the spiritual benefit of writing the vision and making it plain.

In the Book of Ezra lies the prophecy that Jeremiah spoke from the Lord. This story is a classic example of how writing the vision of God and how He will stir the spirit of men and women in authority to consider the plan you have written even if it has been on the shelf for years. I found this to be one story that transcends time and should compel you to write the vision as God commanded King Cyrus.

Ezra wrote:

"Now in the first year of Cyrus king of Persia - in order to fulfill the word of the Lord spoken by the prophet Jeremiah - the Lord stirred up the spirit of King Cyrus king of Persia, so that he sent a proclamation throughout his kingdom, and also **put it in writing** *, saying, thus says Cyrus king of Persia, The Lord, and God, king of heaven, has given me all the kingdoms of the earth, and He* **has appointed** *me to build Him a house in Jerusalem, which in Judah. Whoever there is among you of all his people, may the Lord his God be with him, and let him go up!"* **(2 Chronicles 36:23, bold emphasis mine).**

Two key components correlate with King Cyrus' statement. He said, **"put it in writing"** and he wrote: "He has **appointed** me to build." As we carefully examine the outcome of this proclamation, we will observe how years later the succeeding king (Darius) demanded to see the original written decree that allowed him to enforce, provide, and completely finance the rebuilding of the wall and house of God. This same principle is still used today with most successful plans.

Furthermore, when leadership changes, plans may be altered, but if the plan is clear, concise, and productive, then it will still be effective and bring success in its appointed time. Again, I must stress one more time the importance of "putting it in writing." This principle is such a serious one that God 'Himself' even wrote His vision and gave it to Moses, He wrote:

"Now the Lord said to Moses, "Cut out for yourself two stone tablets like the former ones, and I will write on the tablets the words that were on the former tablets which you shattered" **(Exodus 34:1).**

Once we have received the vision and Word from God, we must write it down. God operates in an **appointed time** principle and if we fail to respond, He has delegate the the plan to someone else who hears His voice. What a shame to ignore the Creator of the heavens and earth. Oftentimes, we assume we haven't heard from God by doubting the vision, or we refuse to write the plan or don't care because we are too busy with our own agenda, which will end in failure or *disappointment*. Why? Because we missed God's APPOINTMENT!!

My computer dictionary defines **writing** as a: Script, symbols, letters, inscriptions, lettering, marks, and characters. When God gives us a vision, it is always trans-generational because it takes the people of each generation to accomplish their phase of it. *If your vision does not transcend your life, its not from God* ...

If it's from you, when you die so will the vision. The word *appointed* is synonymous with chosen, selected agreed, fixed, prearranged, and allotted.

The rebuilding of the temple had ceased for many years until another king began to reign. King Cyrus' vision spoke years later through the spirit of God, because it was ordained and appointed and "did not lie." Without a written proclamation, the new king would not have been able to impose the former decree.

Ezra wrote:

They sent a report to him in whom it was written thus: To Darius the king, all peace. "Let it be known to the king that we have gone to the province of Judah, to the house of the great God, which is being built with huge stones, and beams are being laid in the walls; and this work he is going on with great care and is succeeding in their hands. Then we asked those elders and said to them thus, 'Who issued you a decree to rebuild this temple and to finish this structure?'

Thus they answered 'We are the servants of the God of heaven and earth and we are rebuilding the temple that was built many years ago, which a great king of Israel built and finished. 'But because of our fathers had provoked the God of heaven to wrath, He gave them into the hand of Nebuchadnezzar king of Babylon, the Chaldean, who destroyed this temple and deported the people to Babylon. However, in the first year of Cyrus king of Babylon, King Cyrus issued a decree to rebuild the house of God (**Ezra 4:7-13**).

The importance of writing the vision is not only for **now**, but also when it's presented to someone in the future with the authority to make decisions and influences those in power and positions to consider accepting those plans in their appointed time. The new king, Darius, had no prior knowledge of the decree, but notice how God stirred up the heart and spirit of King Darius to bring what He had commanded and appointed to come to pass.

Ezra wrote:

*Then King Darius issued a decree, and search was made in the archives, where the treasures were stored in Babylon. In Ecbatana in the fortress, which is in the providence of media, a scroll was found and there it was written in it as follows: Memorandum: "In the first year of King Cyrus, Cyrus the king issued a decree: "**Concerning** the house of God at Jerusalem, let the temple the place where sacrifices are offered, be rebuilt and let its foundation be retained, its heights being 60 cubits and its width 60 cubits; with three layers of huge stones and one layer of timbers. And let the cost be paid from the treasury. 'Also let the gold and silver utensils of the house of God Nebuchadnezzar took from the temple in Jerusalem and brought to Babylon, be returned and brought to their places in the temple in Jerusalem; and you shall put them in the house of God.*

So, Darius sent this message: "Now therefore, Tattenai, governor of the province beyond the river Shethar-bozenal and your colleagues, the officials of the provinces beyond the River, keep away from there. "Leave this work on the house of God alone; let the governor of the Jews and the elders of the Jews rebuild this house of God on its site. "Moreover, I issue a decree concerning what you are to do for these elders of Judah in the rebuilding of this house of God: The full cost is to be to these people from the royal treasury out of the taxes of the provinces beyond the river and that without delay." "Whatever is needed, both young bulls, rams, lambs, for burnt offering to the God of heaven, and wheat, salt, wine and anointing oil as the priest in Jerusalem request, it is to be given to them daily without fail, that they may offer acceptable sacrifices to the God of heaven and pray for the life of the king and his sons." "And I issue a decree that any man who violates this edict, a timber shall be drawn from his house he shall be impaled on it and his house shall be made a refuse heap on account of this. May the God who has caused His name to dwell there overthrow any person who attempts to change it as to destroy this house of God in Jerusalem. I Darius have issued this decree; let it be carried out with all diligence!" **(Ezra 6:1-12, bold emphasis mine).**

Notice King Darius' last words, He said, "With all diligence." The need for diligence is a must. Neglecting to write your vision is the primary reason why most people live a sub-par life of happenstance. Again, you can never estimate or underestimate the power of God. It is He that stirs the hearts of men and women to inspire them to show favor even when what they are doing does not make sense. When people have your plan in front of them, they have the opportunity to examine it, and "it" time to speak to them. As God told Habakkuk, **"It will speak and not lie."**

For example, in most business environments a proposal is a **plan** you are presenting to assist a company or person with a future or present project. It is comparable to a vision.

Numerous times in my Telecom Business I was urged by customers to submit a proposal immediately. Surprisingly, after submitting it and occasionally, I wouldn't receive a response from the companies even after inquiring about the proposals or to be told to wait! However, a year later or even longer I would get a call—often from a different person in those companies and be awarded the project.

That proposal (plan) still spoke and did not lie to the customers. The fascinating conclusion about the year-plus of *waiting* is that usually the original cost of the project increased in revenue; thereby resulting in more profit for our company! Isn't that God!!

The Phenomena: King Darius wrote:

*"Moreover, I issue a decree concerning what you are to do for these elders of Judah in the rebuilding of this house of God: The **full cost** is to be to these people from the royal treasury out of the taxes of the provinces beyond the river and that without delay"*

(Ezra 6:8, emphasis in bold mine).

God does not want us concerning ourselves with where the resources will come from. When God gives you a plan, it will be equal to the level of faith you have to bring it to pass. He will never present something to you that you aren't capable doing. As you move through the manifestation of each phase, He always provides *in full* what is needed for you to give your *tithes,* and *offerings* (acceptable sacrifices) *daily* as He did in this story. He also gives what's needed to continue to the next stage of the plan. It is our pride, ego, and greed that cause our plans to falter because we moved outside of God's original plan for us, which will result in delays, losses, or imminent failures.

King Darius continued:

"Whatever is needed, both young bulls, rams, lambs, for burnt offering

to the God of heaven, and wheat, salt, wine and anointing oil as the priest in Jerusalem request, it is to be given to them daily without fail, that they may offer acceptable sacrifices to the God of heaven and pray for the life of the king and his sons" **(Ezra 6:9-10)**.

God's promises are based on our ability to believe what He has said. He moves the spirit of men and women to accomplish His desires for your life. When you **submit the plans** of God's vision to Him, and He accepts it, it becomes His obligation to provide **fully and daily** what is needed to accomplish it.

He told you to "Write the vision."

For instance, when my customers or prospects invite me to assist with their vision, I will ask certain questions to get an understanding of what they want. I write the vision and make it plain. I go to my office and implement (personnel, materials, cost, time-line, etc...) a plan to make the vision a reality for the customers. I submit the plan to the customers and await approval, they accept it, we agree. Now, the customers give me the (check) provisions to get their vision started. Notice, I don't have to worry about where I will get the resources to start the project: This is how God and man work.

God's Vision	Man's Vision
1. God tells vision	1. Man tells vision
2. You write and make plain	2. You write and make plain
3. You create plan	3. You create plan
4. You submit plan to God	4. You submit plan to man
5. God accepts plan	5. Man accepts plan
6. God stirs the heart of man to give the resources	6. Man gives the resources

Darius continued:

"Moreover, I issue a decree concerning what you are to do for these elders of Judah in the rebuilding of this house of God: The **full cost** *is to be to these people from the royal treasury out of the taxes of the provinces beyond the river and that without delay"* **(Ezra 6:8, bold emphasis mine).**

What if I did not submit a plan back to my customers? What happens if you do not submit your plan back to God, today? By writing the vision God has shown you, it is merely His plan. He wants you to present it back to Him with a solution to get the vision done. Once accepted it's a contract between you and God that obligates Him to provide *fully and daily* in order to accomplish it.

In essence, you are writing Gods Words on tablets and waiting for Him to consummate His Word with your faith. As you write the vision and agree with what God has shown you, it has to come to pass because it's a guaranteed contract!

My computer defines proposal as: a plan, scheme, pitch, suggestion, offer, tender, application, or bid. These terms should be enough to compel you to "write that vision." As often as we have been told to "write the vision," most people never do, thereby, prolonging any major success they may have or had now, and in the future. Again, not writing your vision assures you a life of absolute mediocrity, disorganization, disarray, or most likely failure.

Writing Down Your Visions and Goals

A goal setting study sponsored by the Ford Foundation found the following interesting statistics: 23% of the populations have no idea what they want from life and as a result they float around aimlessly.

67% of the population has a general idea of what they want but they don't have any plans for how to get it.

Only 10% of the population has specific well-defined goals but even then, 7 out of 10 of those people reach their goals only half (50%) of the time.

The top 3% of the people in the study achieved their goals 89% of the time. What made the difference for the top 3% who achieved their goals 89% of the time?

They found that of all the possible variables ... the only difference between the top performers and the rest was that the top 3% **wrote down their goals.**

If you study the habits of successful people, you will find that they are organized and planning conscience. *Inc. Magazine* published this article recently stating that **In most cases,** *entrepreneurs begin tackling the challenge of writing a business plan before the business exists.*

Doing that, of course, means that your plan will focus much more on the potential of the business and how you, as the entrepreneur, plan to take advantage of those opportunities (Darren Dahl).

Most successful people will always have their plans and strategies detailed with time lines for meeting them. In closing, I pray that you will not neglect to stop everything you are doing and "write the vision" or go and retrieve the ones you have already written!
The apostle Paul wrote:

"For I say, through the grace given unto me, to every man that is among you, not to think of himself more highly than he ought to think, but to think soberly, according as God hath dealt to every man the measure of faith" **(Romans 12:3).**

The word *soberly* means: severely, sternly, seriously, gravely, and rigorously. This gift of Faith is not just from some associate. It is from God and must be handled with the utmost urgency and care.

My analogy of a measure of faith is: God is so Big that He has put inside each of us (7 billion people estimated in 2015) a piece of Himself (our Faith) as we swipe our barcodes of Faith through prayer He downloads visions, information, directions, instructions, ideas, and inventions from His vast warehouse of infinite knowledge, wisdom, and creative resources. He has created you and me to accomplish His vision for our lives and requires us through faith in Him to manifest these things in an appointed time and season.

God's Appointed Time
Transitions Your Faith into Action

King Solomon gives a wonderful discourse of God's appointed time. He wrote that there is an appointed time for everything.

1. *And there is a time for every event under heaven.*

2. *A time to give birth and time to die; A time plant and a time to uproot what has been planted.*

3. *A time to kill and a time to heal; A time to tear down and a time to build up.*

4. *A time to weep and a time to laugh; A time to mourn and a time to laugh.*

5. *A time to throw stones and a time to gather stones; a time to embrace and time to shun embracing.*

6. *A time to search and a time to give up as lost; a time to keep and a time to throw away.*

7. *A time to tear apart and a time to sew together; a time to be silent and a time to speak.*

8. *A time to love and time to hate; A time for war and a time for peace.*

9. *What profit is there to the worker from that in which he toils?*

10. *I have seen the task with which God has given the sons of men with which occupy themselves. He has made everything appropriate in its time. He has also set eternity in their heart, yet so that man will not find out the work with which God has done from the beginning even to the end* (**Ecclesiastes 3:1-11**).

Kairos Time (Moments)

Solomon's depiction of God's specific allocation of opportunity or missed opportunity of appointed time is predicated upon man's ability to discern the inevitability of reserved moments created for him in the now! Appointed times (Kairos Moments) are those God ordained times that we meet our purpose and destiny to fulfill the sacredness of our creation. Kairos moments are so critical that those closest to us who are there for accountability and guidance will usually recognize these divine occasions too.

You may not be aware of your Kairos moment and have to be pushed into moving forward in it. The Bible gives the most descriptive example of one of the greatest Kairos moments known to mankind: Jesus literally had to be thrust into His destiny by His mother.

The apostle John wrote:

On the third day there was a wedding in Cana of Galilee, and the mother of Jesus was there; and both Jesus and His disciples were invited to the wedding. When the wine ran out, the mother of Jesus said to Him, "They have no wine." And Jesus said to her, "Woman, what does that have to do with us? My hour has not yet come." His mother said the servants, 'Whatever He has said to you do it." Now there were six stone waterpots set there for the Jewish custom for purification, containing twenty or thirty gallons each. Jesus said to them, "Fill the waterpots with water." So they filled them up to the brim. And He said to them, 'Draw some out and take it to the headwaiter." So they took it to him. When the headwaiter tasted the water which had become wine, and did not know where it came from (but the servants who had drawn the water knew), the headwaiter called the bridegroom, and said to him, "Every man serves the good wine first, and when the people have drunk freely, then he serves the poorer wine; but you have kept the good wine until now." This beginning of His signs Jesus did in Cana of Galilee, and manifested His glory, and His disciples believed in Him (John 2:1-11).

After 30 years of preparation and training Jesus finally accepted this moment as His appointed time. Although, He was reluctant, He would not miss it... Those who love, protect, and mentor you will most likely recognize this time before you except it as a Kairos moment of divine purpose for you. You may have to be pushed forward into your destiny as Jesus was by His mother Mary.

Be very cognizant of those unfamiliar with your spirit and purpose and who do not know you well enough to advise you. They will usually mislead you unless they are truly God sent. Jesus' mother knew that this was His Kairos moment and would not allow Him to miss it. The Greeks studied time methodically and mythically, and derived at two dimensions of its existence. Time itself moves forward!! It does not stand idle or move backwards.

They called the first **Kairos**, meaning: now! (I will give several diverse meanings of this powerful, in-the-now word). It is an ancient Greek word meaning: the right or opportune time and moment (The Supreme Moment). The second is **Kronos,** which I will discuss briefly. However, this is a "now" moment, So, I will keep moving forward in it!!

Another meaning for **Kairos** is the fullness of time: God's time zone. Kairos time conveys **notions**, which is synonymous with ideas, philosophy, thinking, accepted wisdom, planning, concept, and design. I must reiterate the need for you to seize it now!

A Kairos moment encompasses much of what we need to activate the plan of God for our destinies. Kairos time is very difficult to measure, for it allows us to move forward in the moment of divine opportunity. We must make careful decisions concerning how we spend this God appointed and ordained time. It must be consumed in the preparation and execution of moving forward toward the vision, period! Kairos moments, they must be seized! Those who are lazy, fearful, asleep, or dull of hearing will miss their Kairos moment with God.

Kronos Time

Kairos moments are to be used with the uttermost vigor and pursuit. You must not allow these precious waves of divine time slots to escape gradually into its counterpart Kronos Time. The Greek mythologists observed and studied time like no other culture. They were responsible for many philosophies surrounding time and the use and myths of it.

The word Kronos is derived from Cronus, the Titan god of time and the ages. They were especially cautious regarding time because they regarded it as destructive and all-devouring. Kronos time does not compel the priority toward destiny and purpose, but according to Greek philosophy, time was measured in seconds, minutes, hours, days, weeks, months, and years. Much different from Kairos, Kronos is cyclical, seasonal, and devoid of urgency in order to accomplish God's purpose for us in His ordained moment of appointed time.

The Grecians, however, respected both Kairos and Kronos time and were extremely adamant about discovering the science of their systems and how both complimented the universe.

We are commanded "*To occupy (do business) until Christ returns*" (Luke 13:19). God never wants us wasting time in any capacity, let alone missed opportunities because we neglect to move forward and capture the moment. In reality, every minute of wasted time is self-destructive and has dire consequences. We must not allow these precious ticks of life to vanish from our inventory of reserve moments. We must capture time as opportunity, value it by our ability to harness the hidden power of it in the heavens, and be wise enough to recognize and master the art of its fleeting existence. David, a man after God's own heart, wrote:

"Teach us to number our days, that we may present you a heart of wisdom" **(Psalm 90:12)**.

Can you imagine how much time you've squandered worrying about what has happened in the past? And wondered why you did not move forward toward your future? How many seconds have turned into minutes and minutes into hours and hours into days and days into weeks and weeks into months and months into years of loss productivity, because of our past failures and disappointments? Our days are numbered and each minute we take for granted is permitting the 'Creative Breath of God' inside each of us to escape without employing the most powerful source known to man, His Spirit!

I pray this day, that not another second of time will escape the mastery of creation God formed you to be, that you decide now, to write the vision and make it plain, move forward; occupy (do business) until Christ returns, by utilizing God's appointed time to transition your faith into action for your purpose and destiny.

Chapter Four
The Foundation of Faith

The Book of Hebrews provides one of the most definitive interpretations of faith: **"Now faith is the substance of things hoped for, the evidence of things not seen" (Hebrews 11:1).**

Many Bible scholars argue that either Apostle Luke or Apostle Paul wrote this book; however, their literary styles and backgrounds do not lend support to this argument. Authorship has remained a mystery. The Book of Hebrews was written to encourage Hebrew Christians not to return to Judaism, (Mosaic Law) but to continue on the path of faith and salvation through Jesus Christ.

In many texts and passages in the New Testament, the word "faith" can literally be interchanged with Jesus.

The writer states:

"Looking unto Jesus the Author and Finisher of our faith who for the joy that was set before him endured the cross, despising the shame, and is set down at the right hand of the throne of God" **(Hebrews 12:2).**

Faith is perhaps the most misunderstood gift from God. Man's lack of spiritual discernment of this gift can be held responsible for many of his struggles. The defining statement in Hebrews 11:1 is obviously one of the most profound portions of Scripture in the entire Bible. Simply put, faith is what the entire Word of God hinges upon.

The word FAITH is predicated upon your ability to act NOW!! Faith is always, NOW!!

Action: Faith requires that you RESPOND, NOW!!!

This chapter will give basic guidelines, principles, and concepts of faith-building as commanded in the Bible. It will also teach you how to strategically apply these basic components in many areas of your life.

I believe God gave me a 'measured gift' of faith to the point that the word 'Faith' is embedded in my name (Fray White = Faith). Perhaps it is a part of my destiny to teach on the basic tenets of faith. The Word of God certainly has plenty to say about this spiritual fountain from which we are invited to draw. Faith has five fundamental components that are revisited throughout the Bible from Genesis to Revelation. Once we understand these principles of applying faith, we can expect them to work in any area of our lives according to the will of God and His Word.

I feel the practice of unwavering faith is stressed repeatedly throughout the Scriptures in hope that we will ultimately grasp and comprehend its significance. These components or building blocks are outlined later in greater detail however, let's first identify them:

1. Christ-The Chief Cornerstone of Christianity

2. Now - An Indicator for Immediate Action

3. Substance - That We Believe for or Desired Matter

4. Hope -Trust in the Outcome BEFORE Seeing

5. Evidence - Proof or Undeniable Results

Godly faith (God-approved) will work only if His concepts, principles, statutes, and judgments are applied; any other form of faith will lead to eminent failure and /or disaster. You can have faith in something that lacks godliness, and it can come to pass, but it will eventually end in failure or fail to bring lasting fulfillment. Nothing has greater effectiveness or a greater foundation than these five components. Nothing godly will be created without these components being applied and activated.

In 2008, the world experienced a rare economic phenomenon. Numerous circumstances rivaled the most devastating financial crisis our country has ever faced since the Great Depression (1936). Our financial institutions, stock markets, automobile industry, telecommunications, housing markets, and every other industry vital to our world's stability were affected by global economic instability. In the United States and other countries, gold had historically secured our currencies, but governments have bandaged this gargantuan problem by printing (hyper-inflating) more money than we have tangible collateral.

Printed money thrown into a devalued economy only reduces the value of existing money and the savings of those who are fortunate enough to weather the storm. Many people, Christians and non-Christians alike, experienced enormous losses of their life's savings, businesses, properties, and investments. For those of us who study the Scriptures and are able to discern spiritual connection, there are lessons to be learned in this evolution of events.

Man-made calamities are usually forecast in the Bible. In this instance King Solomon seems to have revealed the word for the day. You see, we ignored and violated the very basic precaution Solomon alluded to in the Book Ecclesiastes: *"Cast thy bread upon the waters: for thou shall find it* *after many days. Give a portion to seven, and also to <u>eight; for you do not know what evil shall be upon the earth</u>"* (11:1, NLT, underlined emphasis mine).

King Solomon, wisely offered advice to invest money and talents (gifts) seven and eight ways or have as many income producing endeavors (several streams of revenue). Many trusted in man's so-called wisdom and overlooked this simple, yet profound principle.

Evidently, Solomon followed his own advise because I have not read anywhere in the Bible about King Solomon ever filing bankruptcy. As much as is written about him in the Bible there is no mention of lack of money or resources as one of his problems. Even with responsibility to seven hundred wives and three hundred concubines there is no record of lack or need. Why haven't we practiced his financial principles?

As I have researched the global economic dilemma, it appears our economic woes seemingly started with the world's volatile financial and housing markets spiraling downward in value and gradual increases in crude oil that was mainly controlled and imported from the Middle East (OPEC). Organization of Petroleum Exporting Countries: a collective of countries founded in 1960, who chose to collaborate in order to manage the exportation of their crude oil to the rest of the world.

Because of their ability to adjust production levels, they still—over fifty years later, possess a great deal of influence on the price of oil. However, the major oil companies (Exxon, British Petroleum (BP), Shell, Chevron, Phillips and others...) that refine imported crude oil have literally held the world captive, by charging consumers excessive amounts per gallon and have recorded profits unprecedented in the history of fossil fuel consumption.

They have milked the consumer like spotted fat cows on a desolate farm, and draining every drop of liquidity assets we've stored in our udder's, causing many of us to have only powdered and dried up resources. For example: In 2006, I personally paid $250.00 to fill both of my vehicles with mid-grade gasoline. The price was $5.75 per gallon.

That same year the <u>Big Oil Companies</u> posted profits in the billions of dollars and they still continue to gross comparable numbers. Most family's savings and basic living standards have been drastically affected and their accounts reduced to nearly a zero balance in the bank by greed driven CEO's concerned only with earning personal and corporate profitability for their shareholders. It's been almost six years and gasoline prices still fluctuate like bad weather between changing seasons.

In 2008, as gasoline prices inched their way to staggering numbers never seen before in the United States, the rippling effect of the infamous $6.00 per gallon; to include our private and commercial property values also began dropping like sky-divers from a shiny new airplane. This crisis has caused an international domino effect that have plunged many nations inter-connected to America's economy into financial chaos and has trickled down into each of our households.

There are many other contributors for the mess our world is in, I just wanted to awaken you to the severity of our challenges. The primary reason we are experiencing this demise is spiritual and a lack of righteousness within our nations. However, it is being masqueraded and perpetrated as political-economic indifferences.

It has taken many years to finally experience the looming disaster predicted by financial analyst, economist and prognosticators regarding our economies.

They have screamed from the mountain tops in recent years and now we are on the threshold of fiscal collapse of the middle class income earners. Truthfully speaking, most people in the United States are one or two paychecks from being homeless, debt ridden or bankrupt. Since 2008, Congress has poured a total of $2.8 trillion dollars into the economy in an effort to boost hiring, encourage people's spending again and stabilize industries struggling to stay in operation.

If Christians viewed the recession as opportunity rather than a catastrophic event, we would have capitalized from the enormous injection of capital congress threw into our economy. Unfortunately, the money will eventually end up in the hands and coffers of corporate fat cats and their stockholders. Granted, a minuet sect of faithful, informed, enterprising and capitalistic thinkers will also take full advantage of the enormity of excess cash flowing through our markets. In other words, "The Rich Will Get Richer!"

The majority of the population is relegated by choice into thinking and responding adversely, due to a faithless-consumer oriented mentality, instead of transforming themselves into a venture-capitalist-mode way of thinking to actively participate in the world of commerce. In actuality, we have more money flowing in our economy than before the recession. So, to say it's a recession would be incorrect! I would say, "It's an injection!"

The government gave Christians ample opportunity to prepare for the "Injection" (Stimulus Package). There were people who waited for Congress to vote it into law and had planned and strategized ways to obtain some of the money. Their perception was one of opportunity and not of fear. Our lack of vision and preparation caused many of us to miss an enormous amount of money circulating in our economy to create and build businesses, stabilize families, give to our churches and other endeavors.

Christians must get out from behind the *four walls* of the church and migrate into mainstream society to become relevant contributors   effecting change, by gaining influence and power through business, commerce and government. Many have placed their faith on information not principally sound or godly in nature.

Otherwise, we will become insignificant and obsolete in a culture that is benefiting from using godly principles that are necessary to coexist and fulfill the great commission commanded by Christ. We are to go out into the world and spread the Gospel **(Matthew 28:18)**.

At the same time intellectualism has given rise to an unfortunate movement which seeks to dispel many of the basic godly principles, simple in content but powerful in consequence—outlined throughout the Bible. Ignoring or devaluing God's principles represents a major breach in our heaven-ordained assignment. God gave us the ability to create and a degree of free will, but His principles are not negotiable or compromised. Rather, they are set in stone and not to be dishonored.

Faith is neither complex, nor intellectual. It is the confidence in what God reveals through His word, visions, signs, and dreams. With time and effort (works) faith will bring all things promised to pass. The apostle Mark described Jesus as the Chief Corner Stone. He recalled when Jesus spoke to the Pharisees about "The Parable of the Vineyard" and said:

"Have you not even read this Scripture:*"THE STONE WHICH THE BUILDERS REJECTED, THIS BECAME THE CHIEF CORNER stone, THIS CAME ABOUT FROM THE LORD AND IT IS MARVELOUS IN OUR EYES?"* **(Mark 12: 10-11)**.

The hope we have in Christ as our Chief Cornerstone is totally dependent on the foundation and of our faith. It is not affected by the fluctuating markets of the world's economies, wars, plagues or disasters, but predicated upon our ability to believe the Word of God. A faith-filled Christian does not live in fear of the unknown or unseen, nor does he or she concern themselves with contradictions and futility written by men of limited wisdom, knowledge and understanding of God.

Our divine predictions of the future and world occurrences have been written and predetermined in His Bible before the world began, with absolute precision. Our faith in the Chief Cornerstone has given us an unshakable immortal foundation that is not subject or volatile to earthly conditions, but is built on the immovable sustaining Word of God.

Chapter Five
Faith Building Components

Consider faith-building as an activity similar to early activities with building blocks in nursery school or at home when you were a toddler. It did not necessarily take a lot of blocks to construct something which resembled a house, a skyscraper or a store. The blocks were basic and indeed required some use of the imagination. Likewise the five components of Faith-building can be thought of in similar fashion.

There were other instances in childhood during outside play that we took advantage of the presence of little stones to construct fences, build miniature houses or huts, or to design entire cities or kingdoms.

Let's retrogress for a moment and begin to build a house or temple of faith. Fundamentally, we will need five stones to begin. They are as follows:

1. Christ - Chief Cornerstone
2. Now - Immediate Action
3. Substance - Desired Matter
4. Hope - Trust without or before Seeing
5. Evidence - Proof

Now, let's isolate the stones and examine the specific role each played in building a temple or house of faith—not a physical building but in our existence and spirit.

The Five Stones of Faith

CHRIST

Christ is the first and supreme component. He is the Author and Finisher of our faith. He is the embodiment of our past, present, and future. Without contradiction, He can advise us on any level. He brings both relevance and uniqueness to our lives. His name speaks volumes and moves every obstacle of interference designed to hinder us. Also, He empowers us with grace to withstand any plot of resistance to our plans. Christ knows every turn we must take, at which time and juncture to shift, change, or move ahead. He is the 'Ultimate Progressive Change Agent.'

Unfortunately, many Christians or believers have reduced Christ to a historical symbol and placed Him in the archives of obsolescence. We have downgraded Him to the man on the cross in our churches. We have assigned Him to perch as a marker in cemeteries. And, in older churches in the rural south, He has become the figure on old church hand-held paper fans. However, the moment we view Christ as the forerunner of all creativity and use His teachings as the standard of quality and quantity of all conception then and only then are we postured to realize success beyond measure.

Please allow me to direct your attention to Luke's writings which identify Jesus has the Chief Instructor, wrote:

"Why do you call me, 'Lord, Lord,' and do not do what I say? "Everyone that comes to Me and hears My words and acts on them, I will show you whom he is like: He is a man building a house, who dug deep and laid a foundation on the rock; and when the flood occurred, the torrent burst against that house and could not shake it, because it

had been well built. But the one who has heard and has not acted accordingly, is like a man who built his house on the ground without any foundation; and the torrent burst against it and immediately it collapsed, and the ruin of that house was great" **(Luke 6:46-49).**

The conclusion of every matter concerning creativity is that we might as well come to Christ *first* before later. He will ensure success and His word will be the sure standard and guide for completion. Once the Chief Cornerstone (Christ) is laid as the foundation of our faith, we can begin adding the next four (stones) components. What more is there to say? We're blessed to have Christ on our Team!! Actually, He should be our Captain!

NOW

Webster's defines the second component **Now** as at the present time; at this moment; at once; or very soon. In this sense, now means to believe the very moment! This is what God expects from us. The instant He shows us something (by revelation, inspiration or natural realm) we must believe and put into action (NOW, today) the planning and works necessary for the substance to follow.

Now indicates that we are determined to move forward without first seeing the means (resources) of acquiring the substance, but as you transition toward what you have seen either in the natural or spiritual realm it, will come to pass. Essentially, faith gives us the ability to step into the future and bring back proof of its existence or to see something in the natural realm and lock that object of substance into our spirit until it becomes the evidence of our desire. Many times we fail to identify the substance and that guarantees our faith will be diluted or non-existent.

I will discuss later the importance of the *target* and how to lock it into your being to bring forth any substance over time. The American essayist, lecturer, and poet, stated *"the past or the future, I have nothing to do with, I live in the NOW!"*— Ralph Waldo Emerson

SUBSTANCE

The third component is **Substance** It is defined as the real or essential part or element of anything; essence, reality, or basic matte; the physical matter of which a thing consists, the body or the real content, meaning, or gist of something said or written; material possessions; property; resources; wealth: or something that has independent existence and is acted upon by causes. Again, I will reiterate the last part.... said, written, and acted upon.

You must first have a clear vision of the substance desired. The substance again can be an animate or inanimate object. God will move only when it is in accordance with His will and word. Faith is only relative to the believer's ability to see the desired substance. He is the God of specifics and belief. God does not agree with doubt or fear: you must know what you are hoping for. Each phase of obtaining substance must be accompanied by the specifics of the desired evidence.

According to Hebrews 4:16, the writer, said: *"Let us therefore come boldly to the throne of grace that you may obtain mercy, and find grace to help in time of need."*

These words mean: I must first see (natural or spiritual) what I want before I go to the Holy Father; not in timidity but in boldness that what I am hoping and trusting for will be granted because of His grace and mercy.

HOPE

The fourth component of faith is *Hope* (Future). Which is defined as a desire of some good, accompanied by the **belief** that it is attainable; trust; one in who trust is placed or confidence is placed in the object of hope; to **trust**; or to desire with some expectation of attainment. *Hope* believes in the *Future*, while *Faith* believes in the *NOW!!!*

If you will notice the repetitive mention of the word belief and trust, how they are interrelated with Hope. These three must intrinsically work together with the expectation of receiving the substance. However, you must remove ALL doubt!!

- *Hope* is the belief in the bridge between faith and love.

- *Hope* is the belief in the cement that fortifies your faith.

- *Hope* is the belief in the rope that pulls the weight.

- *Hope* is the belief in the peace that surpasses all understanding.

- *Hope* is the belief in the source of strength that supersedes weakness.

- *Hope* is the belief in the band that secures every crack.

- *Hope* is the belief in the fuel that keeps the lamp lit.

- *Hope* is the belief in the spark that ignites the flame of victory.

- *Hope* is the belief in the navigational system that guides you to your destiny.

- *Hope* is the belief in the stream that continues to flow into the rivers of faith and trust in God.

- *Hope* is the belief in the relationship that Jesus has with God.

- *Hope* is the belief in the power that God sends to us through the Holy Spirit.

Hope, Belief and Trust are the three vital co-components that set in motion the excitement that invokes the Holy Spirit to move within your faith.

Faith in the **NOW...** it ignites the expectation of what is attainable by trusting in God's ability to deliver that which is not seen, but believed.

EVIDENCE

The fifth and last component is **evidence:** Is the finish product of faith. This is where our faith is tried, tested, and proven. Oftentimes, we expect the evidence to manifest instantaneously. If it doesn't, we become doubtful and begin to waiver by not allowing Christ to finish our Faith.

We must not intervene or circumvent the process of maturation in what God is doing to work out the desired evidence. Remember God's words to the prophet Habakkuk. He said: *"Though it tarry waits, for the vision is for an appointed time, it shall speak and not lie"* (Habakkuk2:3). Webster defines **evidence** as: That which demonstrates that a fact is so; testimony; proof; witness; to make evident; and to prove. Evidence is the end product of faith, without it there is no faith.

The faith of a 97- year old woman who once lived at the base of a mountain in California bears witness to this fact. Very often large boulders will become loosened from eroding soil after heavy rains, landslides and earthquakes. In this instance a gigantic boulder, large enough to completely crush the elderly woman's house tumbled all the way down the mountain. A tree, not very large at all, became the resting place of the threatening piece of rock. It stopped the rock just before it landed on her house on its downward journey. Local authorities rushed to her house and informed her that she must evacuate immediately and give them the opportunity to try to find a way to remove the danger. Much to their concern, she refused.

This was her reply: "I have lived for nearly a hundred years. I have faced many trials, dangerous situations, near disasters and serious illness. I have sat in my home and watched boulders fall off this mountain. SOMETHING or SOMEONE has ALWAYS protected me and worked it out without much interference on my part. It took me a minute to realize that I was certainly not responsible for these outcomes. I could have died a long time ago. Now, because I have always had that protection, I don't think I will abandon my FAITH today! Just leave the rock alone. I'll be okay and it will be okay. Just watch!" The lady never left her home and the rock never moved another inch—until after her natural death!

Without a doubt this old lady had encountered God on her life's journey and had learned to trust Him without reservation. In her mind she might have thought that if she ran from this threatening situation, she could easily have run directly into another. I would guess that some of the circumstances she faced in life over the course of nearly a century could have caused her to quit or give up.

More importantly, she did not quit believing! Her faith remained reliant on God and His promise to sustain and keep her. She had lived too long to quit and give up!

Her faith was extraordinary. God's decision to honor her faith was typical of His tendency to keep His promise. The measure of faith God gave her grew abundantly, far beyond that exhibited by most individuals. She based her faith on the evidence of her past, by continually trusting in God to love and protect her.

Faith and Love Never Fails Unless You Quit

God's whole plan for man is rooted in FAITH and LOVE. There is no pleasing Him without them. The power of believing in God and His word is the fiber of our existence. We will never produce anything without first seeing it in our minds (spirit) or in the natural realm and then trusting in what we believe. Faith, love, and action will gradually move the desired substance into existence.

Every person, place, and thing you need will begin to connect supernaturally and collectively for the common cause of producing the desired substance to bring forth the evidence of your faith. Evidence seen can never be denied, for it is the living proof that what you are hoping for by faith and works has happened. Steve Jobs, the late founder of Apple Computer stated:

"Your work is going to fill a large part of your life, and the only way to be truly satisfied is to do what you believe is great work. And the only way to do great work is to love what you do. If you haven't found it yet, keep looking. Don't settle. As with all matters of the heart, you'll know when you find it. And, like any great relationship, it just gets better and better as the years roll on. So keep looking until you find it. Don't settle."

Oftentimes, when our faith is tried, we must reflect on our own history or someone else's (evidence). When God is promoting (stretching) you, it's often accompanied by the testing of your faith. He often allows a major event in your life to occur, causing you to be uncomfortable in the growing of your faith. Your life becomes a challenge and many times unraveled to prepare you for a new journey of faith.

When you quit, the substance of your faith is still moving toward your desires to produce the evidence of what you were hoping for. If you quit, someone else with greater faith will reap the benefits of your unfinished faith. However challenging, you must continue and not turn from what you believe to see a finish product.

Although, you can't see the immediate substance you're hoping for, there is a far greater product of evidence being produced if you don't quit.

Thomas Edison, the great inventor, tried over a 1,000 times to find the right filament for his lighting system. In the process of his attempts, he discovered many other inventions and patented them from his failures.

Mr. Edison quoted: *"Our greatest weakness is giving up. The most certain way to success is to try more time."* - Inventor and Holder of 1,093 U.S. Patents.

Truth: *Failures are only divine discoveries of the hidden mysteries of our finished faith.*

Remember: FAITH and LOVE NEVER FAILS UNLESS YOU QUIT...

I have never failed at anything unless I have quit! Question: How many times have you quit? Your life is exactly at the point where you have quit!!

You *quit* praying

You *quit* meditating on God.

You *quit* listening

You *quit* believing

You *quit* fasting

You *quit* reading the Bible

You *quit* going to Church.

You *quit* being obedient to God's Word.

You *quit* laughing.

You *quit* dreaming.

You *quit* living

You *quit* giving.

You *quit* forgiving.

You *quit* caring.

You *quit* serving.

You *quit* working

You *quit* planning.

You *quit* learning.

You *quit* moving forward.

You *quit* growing.

You *quit* hoping.

Which means: You *quit* loving? Faith gives you the will power to continue towards the desires of your heart. When our hearts are affected by something or someone we love it ignites and feeds the spirit that will not allow us to quit the work until it's complete. Love should be the driving force behind our faith. The apostle Paul expressed the principle of love in his first letter to the Church at Corinth. He wrote:

"Love never fails. But where there are prophecies, they will cease; where there are tongues, they will be stilled; where there is knowledge, it will pass away. For we know in part and we prophesy in part, but when completeness comes, what is in part disappears" (1ˢᵗ Corinthians1:9).

The completeness Paul spoke of is the love Christ has for us. Faith and love will always push you to the finish line.

Truth: Faith has inherent mechanisms of success built into its system that can never fail, unless you stop loving and turn from what you believe.

It is impossible not to succeed if you trust God; if you are in obedience and *you* don't quit. Faith and love will always produce evidence of success if you finish and don't turn from what you see and believe.

Luke describes how your faith can fail if one turns from his faith. He wrote Jesus' statement to Peter:

"Simon, Simon, behold, Satan has demanded permission to sift you like wheat; but I have prayed for you that your faith may not fail; and when you have once turned again, strengthen your brothers"
(Luke 22:31-32).

Oftentimes, all hell will come against you, but you must not turn from your faith. You must believe!! Mark stated it plainly. Jesus said to him:

"As possibilities go, everything is possible for the person who believes" **(Mark 9:23).**

Successful people are successful because they love what they do, they believe, they don't turn, and they finish. They leave secrets of success straight to the finish line! Jesus is the Author and Finisher of our faith. He set the greatest example of finishing at Calvary: As He hung on the cross; there was a jar full of sour wine in the midst of the people. He said, "I'm thirsty." They took a Hyssop branch dipped in the wine, and put it to His mouth, and when He tasted the sour wine, He said, "It is finished."

Jesus knew that if He could only make it to the cross, be nailed, hung, hoisted, and endure the excruciating pain, agony, suffering, and piercing in what would seem an eternity that the people would no longer have to die because of their sins. Jesus accepted the fact that He was the only one capable of accomplishing such an inhumane, undeserving, incompassionate, indecent, and horrendous form of death for a dying world incapable of deserving such a sacrificial act of divine love.

Jesus was determined not to quit and not turn away from those God loves; that have enough faith to trust in Him saying:

"For God so loved the world, that He gave His only begotten Son, that whosoever believes in Him shall not perish but have everlasting life. For God did not send the Son into the world to judge the world, but that the world might be saved through Him" **(John 3:16-17).**

Jesus always wants us to press ahead and finish and not turn from our faith. God expects us always to complete what we start. His love for us made Him create the heavens and earth, and He did not quit until He finished His work each day. Just like the elderly woman in California, I'd like to encourage you to develop a sense of faith which, I admit, might appear "insane" or irrational to others, but she was a classic example of how faith in God's ability to protect her from the fallen rock, she never quit believing and trusting in God's ability to protect her because she knew He Loved her.

God is the ultimate Judge to those who call upon Him. Jesus explained to His disciples how an unrighteous judge, who did not fear God or respect man, responded to a woman who cried out for justice from her opponent; day and night—she would not quit!!

He stated:

"Now, will not God bring about justice for His elect who cry to Him day and night, and will He delay long over them? I tell you that He will bring justice for them quickly. However, when the Son of Man comes, will he find faith on the earth?" **(Luke 18:7-8).**

When Christ returns He expects to find faith visible over all the earth illustrated <u>through</u> His people. The only way this will happen is, if the church is indeed <u>actively living by and exhibiting </u>faith. We must breathe life into the message in the word which states, "So faith comes from hearing, and by hearing the Word of God."

Chapter Six
God's Six Days of Faith through:
Systems, Networks, and Relationships

The word *System* is uniquely related to faith. It is defined as a set of connected things or parts forming a complex whole; in particular things working together as parts of a mechanism or an interconnecting network. God created the heavens and the earth by faith in His word to support His divine creation for man to rule, subdue, and dominate systematically through a network of godly principles and relationships. Faith must have corresponding systems, networks and relationships based on God's word of truth.

God created the lighting system, the solar system, the water system, the eco-system, the resource system (plants and food), and the management system (man). In the Garden of Eden every system, network and relationship was functioning exactly how God created it to work. It was an orderly environment where man was one with God. Adam tended to the day-to-day activities of the Garden.

The love for his wife Eve made his responsibilities an effortless endeavor, for his every pleasant thought of passion for her consumed his mind. The presence of the Spirit of God walking in the cool of the day in complete harmony and in divine relationship with them was comforting.

Nature was in complete order with the universe: the stars, the sun, the moon, the seas, the trees, the animals, and man were all occupying, congregating, and flourishing in unity and in peace. A heavenly-harmonic and symphonic sound resonated so beautifully throughout the Garden, as the multiplicity of exotic animals and species sang rhythmically together, making joyous sounds that emanated from their activities of pleasure. They freely crept, crawled, flew, swam, swung, ran, and roamed in the Botanical Garden of Paradise.

They ate, played, and enjoyed the abundance of lush vegetation that satisfied their palates. The Garden was watered from a glistering-streaming crystal clear river that divided into four beautifully divinely flowing tributaries named the Pishon, Gihon, Tigris, and Euphrates. And the underground water system that encompassed the surrounding regions.

It was all created by God. Eve was a beautiful woman of intrigue, curiosity, inquisitiveness, and adventure. She often wondered liberally, occasionally admiring the opulence of precious stones and the abundance of fine gold scattered indiscriminately throughout the Garden. Her longing to discover the origin of this vast oasis of beauty caused her to question the validity of its existence.

She couldn't fathom the thought of such a place of splendor having limitations and restrictions and violated her relationship with God; by believing the doubting gesture of a menacing-stranger-of-low-degree to the point, she convinced the man she loved to doubt His authority, too! Oh, how that old serpent lied to Eve.

The act of uncertainty, disobedience, and contempt changed their whole systems, networks, relationships, and faith forever. In the twinkling of an eye! In a brief encounter of a vague and subtle suggestion! In a moment of ominous questions and answers, where two lovers meet, in deceit to eat! And finally, in an act of a lie! Their paradise suddenly became a place of enmity, a place of hiding, a place of danger, and a place of protection and self- preservation from every species of creation to include each other. Their decision changed their relationship with God and set in motion a trans-generational consequence for all mankind.

Our paradise becomes a remnant of what Eden was when we institute a false system of faith in our network based on lies or doubt. Our *faith, systems, networks,* and *relationships* will cease to work for us when lies or doubt are present. Our casual, passive, and general spoken words of lies or doubt will hinder, deny, or destroy the process of godly evidence and the trans-generational concept God mandates. Our thinking, speaking and planning should always be to create a godly legacy based on truth that will remain long after we are gone.

If you study the success of some religious institutions, worldly empires, and dynasties they have inter-woven systems, networks, and relationships of faith that transcend generations. However, if those systems are not built on the foundation of truth, they will eventually crumble.

A **Network** is a supportive system of sharing information and services among individuals and groups having a common interest. These three faith activating components must work cohesively together to form that interconnecting purpose in truth to grow your faith.

It is crucial that you understand their meanings and purpose. Michael Hicks Director of Information Technology at Paine College in Augusta, GA stated, "If you are not networking today, you will not be working tomorrow!" In 2012, this was the general consensus at the Educause Leadership Conference held in Indianapolis, IN.

A *Relationship* is the way in which two or more concepts, objects, or people are connected. Adam and Eve's disobedience certainly changed the relationship they had with God when he succumbed to a lie and doubted the Word of God.

Below are the categories of examples within the Systems, Networks and Relationships we must incorporate into our lives to become faithful and productive Christians.

Truth: Your success and future depends on you developing these components. You must incorporate these core principles into your System (Core Foundation)

1. God, Jesus and Holy Spirit

2. Love

3. Family (Biological, Adopted or Christian)

4. Righteousness

5. Work and Business

6. Morals

7. Ethics

8. Truth

9. Values

10. Integrity

11. Security

12. Education

Networks (Organizations, Associations and Affiliations)
1. Church (Serving)
2. Charitable Endeavors (Volunteering)
3. Fraternities and Sororities
4. Clubs
5. Professional Associations (Related to job or business)
6. Foundations
7. Mentoring
8. Counseling
9. Bartering
10. Partnerships
11. Conferences
12. Lectures

Relationships
1. Friends (Love)
2. Sports
3. Hobby's
4. Vacations
5. Special Occasions
6. Gatherings
7. Support
8. Trust
9. Confidant
10. Transparency
11. Laughter and Weeping
12. Listening

There are many other tangible words I could use for these three components however, the few listed above are a microcosm of essentials needed for our faith to grow and work. God used all three of these components when He created the earth. We must use them as well to create our lives and sustain them through faith and truth. God did not create us to act alone. When I am confronted with a challenge or need some form of assistance I can depend on my systems and networks to derive at a solution, because I have cultivated and maintained value-added relationships into my life as well as theirs.

If you do not develop and implement these three components into your life you will NEVER live a life of success because you need people to help you accomplish your visions and goals through faith—your systems, networks and relationships and they must be based on truth. Recently, we have experience a plethora of scandals that have expose the lying society we are becoming.

This type of dishonest behavior is affecting, religion, government, politics, business, entertainment, media, our judicial system, and family in every sphere of our society and lives imaginable. Our great-grandparents, grandparents, parents, uncles, aunts, brothers, sisters, nephews, nieces, kids, friends and associates have become professional liars and effectively have no power to create godly change. Today our presidents, pastors, teachers, public servants, doctors, lawyers, and other authority figures will say whatever is fashionable for the moment.

In essence, we are all speaking words that will not return unto us void. We often don't have any intentions of fulfilling the words we have spoken, which cause our systems of faith to fail, and God cannot be involved. God desires to give to us what we pray or hope for, but our faith must be based on His word of truth.

Jesus said:

"If you abide in Me and My words abide in you, ask whatever you wish, and it will be done for you" (John 15:7).

The faith God wants us to use must expand beyond our imperfect capacity and reach into the spiritual world that has no limits or boundaries and is based on truth. Our words will always shape our future and the generations that follow. God's word always produces the very thing that He speaks.

We are made in His image and whatever we say—whether we like it or not can or will eventually happen in our lives. Godly faith never lies or doubts! God spoke every system, network, and relationship into existence by faith in His word and never said another word, but He saw that it was good or very good (Genesis1:3-31).

Day 1: God Created Everything with Words of Truth *(Systems and Networks)*

IN THE beginning God (prepared, formed, fashioned, and) created the heavens and the earth. The earth was without form and an empty waste, and darkness was upon the face of the very great deep. The Spirit of God was moving (hovering, brooding) over the face of the waters. And God said, Let there be light; and there was light. And God saw that the light was good (suitable, pleasant) and He approved it; and God separated the light from the darkness. And God called the light Day, and the darkness He called Night. And there was evening and there was morning, one day (Genesis 1:5).

God meticulously and methodically began calling the systems into existence with truth. I believe that most often our faith doesn't work because of the compromises of truth in the systems of our networks and in our relationships.

You will never accomplish God's desires for your life if it's built on lies or doubt. My faith grew exponentially, and my relationships abounded as my doubts became less and I kept my word (spoke truth). It was only when I began to doubt or lie to my network of relationships that my faith systems began to fail, and people lost faith in me.

That's why when people say, "I have faith in that man or woman because they do exactly what they say." At any time, we can become successful in whatever God desires for us to do, but faith must start with truth. The moment we introduce lies or doubt into the equation our faith becomes compromised, and we will not see godly evidence of His desire for our life.

We have convoluted this godly principle of truth by being permissively tolerant in allowing the integration of the subtlety of lies and doubt into the plans of God for our lives. Our nations have become nations of liars and doubters. We will lie at the drop of a dime and not have any feelings of remorse or moral consciousness. God cannot participate nor will He where there is not truth and trust. Our confidence in God and His word must be unquestionable. You can be sure that what He says is going to happen will happen. The Bible says:

"God is not like people. He tells no lies. He is not like humans. He doesn't change his mind. When he says something, he does it. When he makes a promise, he keeps it" (**Numbers 23:19, GWT**).

For godly faith to work, we must always speak truth and never lie or doubt. In today's society our promises mean absolutely nothing, and that is the primary reason why we see very little evidence of godly signs, wonders, and miracles.

Warning: There will not be <u>lasting</u> God ordained evidence with lies or doubt as a foundation! God will have nothing to do with lies or doubt. I challenge you to start speaking the truth in every area of your life and watch your systems, networks, and relationships of faith began to be restored. They will begin to grow with signs, wonders, and miracles.

Lies We Speak Will Return Unto Us

1. I will call you back in 10 minutes. But you rarely do (Often tell our friends).

2. I, He or She is not home (We tell bill collectors: answer the phone they will work with you).

3. Tell them I am not here (We tell our kids to lie).

4. I love you, but I'm not in-love with you (To people we use, more in chapter 10).

5. I was out with the boys or girls (Cheaters).

6. I did not see your text (We tell our associates).

7. My phone is not working (Ignoring people).

8. I will try to make it (No plans to come at all).

9. The Spirit told me to do this (Holy Spirit or yours?)

10. We are just testing our love: living together (shacking) before marriage; usually ends in divorce or never committing or long term pain for either or both parties).

11. I'm going do this or that one day... (Church folk still doing what the Children of Israel did) Don't' let 11 days turn into 40 years. <u>Do it NOW!</u>

12. God is punishing me (No He isn't! Those lies are returning unto you).

Of course, there are thousands of other lies we tell and most of us aren't even aware of the consequences of our words.

Jesus said we will be held accountable. Matthew stated this plainly:

*"The good man brings out of **his** good treasure what is good; and the evil man brings out of **his** evil treasure what is evil "But I tell every careless word that people speak, they shall give an accounting for it in the day of judgment. "For by your words you will be justified, and by your words you will be condemned"*
(Matthew 12:35, bold emphasis mine).

The Bible says, "The earth was dark and had no form." Then the Spirit of God (Holy Spirit) moved upon the depths observing and waiting for a command. God said, "Let there be light," and there was light. He spoke the light from the darkness. He created something from total darkness with His words. We all have the ability to create things by faith and our works. As we apply God's word as the foundation of godly faith and follow His principles and wisdom, we should never doubt that what we speak will not manifest. We will say it, examine it, name it, call it very good, and assume full authority over what is created.

Before God began creating the heavens and the earth, both were one big mass consumed and covered by water. According to the Bible, it was completely dark, void, and without form. As we carefully examine this process, we will see how God began framing and laying out the foundation of creation by His Word. First, one must realize that before God could say "Let there be light," light had to be in God and then a thought in His mind...

It is extremely important that we observe these patterns of events. On the first day, God said, "Let there be light," and there was light. Note: God is light, the light emanated to His mind, and it became a reality. For creation to occur what will be created must first occupy your mind and through manifestation of your thoughts it can gradually appear by works.

God divided the light from the darkness with an authoritative command to His Holy Spirit, which resulted in the appearance of what He wanted. Afterwards, He inspected it, saw that it was good, and called the light "Day" and the darkness He called "Night."

It is vitally important that we understand the need to name what we create. In early times, when someone conquered a city or settled in that city, the conquerors often named or renamed the place after the leader as a symbol of control, dominion over their conquest, or as the founder. Those founders word would become the supreme rule, and they could create whatever system, government, and society they desired. Even today, inventors name what they create or control the naming of their product. Cities and streets all over the world are named after people that influenced those cities and have or had prominence in those areas.

In the Garden of Eden, God formed each animal out of the dust. He brought each animal to Adam to see what he would name them. Whatever Adam said is what they were (Genesis 2:19). Adam was given dominion over the Garden; therefore, he could call them whatever he wanted. God ordains these commands and principles. However, He does not approve control over people. God expects leaders to govern His people with love, wisdom, and knowledge based on His Word.

Day 2: Systems and Networks

God began the second day by separating the waters: Then He said, "Let there be an expanse (space between e a r t h and heaven) in the midst of the waters, and let it separate the waters from the waters." God made the expanse and separated the waters, which were below the expanse. He made the water to gather together in one place. He spoke and the dry land it appeared. He called the dry land earth, and the gathering of the waters He called Seas. God saw that it was good **(Genesis 1:6-10)**.

This concluded the second day of His creation. Now, it was time for God to start speaking life-sustaining components from the earth. You must speak life into your dreams and visions once you see them. I have a habit of talking to myself constantly to remind myself of my dreams. Hearing myself encourages me to stay focused on the target. I do not care if anyone agrees with me or how far-fetched my ideas seem: I do not care what man thinks. When God gives me a vision, why would I be concerned about what anyone thinks? Although, you may not see the end of your vision, the fun and excitement are bringing what part you see, saying to yourself "very good."

I don't believe in reinventing the wheel. If there is a working template or model of what I see, then I realize I must do something comparable or greater to obtain and maintain it. For instance, if I am an NBA basketball player who wants to score 30 points every night, I must study the player or players who score 30 points each night. If I am not willing to do the work behind the scene when I am not playing, in practice, studying opponents, conditioning, diet, and other intangibles, more than likely, I will never accomplish this goal. I repeat: *I will never accomplish this goal!* This principle must be applied in every sphere of life.

Faith must have a sound foundation. It must be principled in understanding and knowledge of the endeavor. Solomon wrote:

"Without counsel purposes are disappointed: but with the multitudes of counselors they are established" (**Proverbs 15:22**)

As we continue to study the six days of creation, notice how God built upon each foundation and how one supported the others systematically. Faith should also have thought and details that support the foundation of substance, for this concept is core to the success of your vision. God is the greatest planner in the universe, and it is remarkable how we overlook these basic principles when planning our vision. He did not give them to us to shelve. Instead, your plans must be cultivated daily and measurably in order to bring them to fruition.

In these six days, there were no delays in the daily process of completing each task. We too, must work on our vision daily (except on our rest day) until we get to the next level of manifestation. We will receive the next phase of the vision as we complete the previous one.

Peter said:

"One day in the Lord is like a thousand years" (**2 Peter 3:5**).

Day3: Systems and Networks

God divided the waters and separated them, and the earth appeared. Then God said, "Let the earth bring forth grass and herbs yielding seed" God began to supply His earth by *calling* plants yielding seed, fruit trees with seeds to reproduce after its kind from the earth and vegetation yielding its seed after its kind.

"And the earth brought forth fruit trees, vegetation, and plants yielding seed and God saw that it was good" **(Genesis 1:11-13)**.

This ends the third day. It's imperative that you study this day in particular. The Bible says, "He called forth these plants and vegetation from the earth." God's faith is in action, systematically laying out the earth and its networks and putting each in the correct order and time. Just as God called these plants out of the earth, your gifts are lying dormant within you waiting to be called out of you at their appointed time. Remember Habakkuk 2, *"Though it tarry wait, it will speak and not lie."*

The third day is extremely interesting. It reveals a critical truth that we often neglect. I will add a twist and say: "this is why trees and plants still grow upward today, continuously towards heaven, because they still obey God's voice." We are the only creation that has a problem obeying His commands.

The third day establishes a fact that nothing will fall from the sky. When we get this concept in our heart, evidence will never again elude the faithful. Then God said, "Let the earth bring forth it plants, trees, and vegetation with seed yielding" (reproducing substance).

Everything we desire will come from the earth. At your command earth and man will bring forth the substance we are hoping for. It will follow your voice as it did God's. This godly principle should not be as difficult to grasp, but most falter here. The one thing you do not observe is God negating (doubting) the expectation of evidence. He could have if He had said anything contrary to what was first spoken. "And God said!"

What are you saying? Whatever you have said or are saying or believed or what was said about you is the life you are now living. The moment lies or unbelief (doubt) is spoken to you, about you or from you the process of godly evidence for your life can be hindered or completely aborted.

In the Book of Proverbs, Solomon wrote:

"Death and life are in the power of the tongue and they that love it shall eat the fruit thereof" **(Proverbs 18:21)**.

Solomon is basically saying, "You will possess the fruit or substance you confess or believe." God's substance manifested because He never saw it any other way than it "good and very good." The third day should be studied and dissected to get the essence of how the earth will provide everything we need for our natural bodies while God will provide for our spiritual needs. If believers can get this principle into their heart, nothing will be impossible for those who will believe.

God wants Christians to manifest what appears to be impossible to glorify Him and His Son. We must stop looking for substance to be manifested from God and understand that His earth will provide everything we need based on what we see, imagine, speak, and believe according to God's will—by faith. Contrary to some prognosticators, we will never deplete God's resources.

Moses wrote: *"While the earth remains, seedtime and harvest, and cold and heat, and summer and winter and day and night shall not cease"* **(Genesis 8:22)**.

God will give us new ideas, visions, dreams, and signs through the Holy Spirit. He will show us how to cultivate and bring forth enhancements and other benefits from His earth, but they will not fall from the sky. What you desire will come from the earth and through man.

Solomon wrote:

"History merely repeats itself. It has all been done before. Nothing under the sun is truly new. Some people say, "Here is something new!" But actually it is old; nothing is ever truly new. We don't remember what happen in the past and in the future generations, no one will remember what we are doing now"(**Ecclesiastes 1:9-11,NLT**).

We will never create something new, but only enhance or improve that which has already been created. Our prayers, therefore, should be to enhance or improve what is already created.

Day 4: Systems and Networks

God said, "Let there be lights in the expansion to separate the day and the night and for the signs and for seasons and for days and for years. And let them give light in the heavens and on earth, and it was so" (Genesis 1:14-15). God made these great lights to rule. We are to rule as lights of Christ. He made greater light to rule the day and the lesser to rule the night. He also made the stars. These divided the day from night and let them be for signs, seasons, days and years. Again, God saw that it was good. This is God's way of setting time and seasons.

These are the systems needed to sustain the next phase of creation. Notice, carefully, the foundational process of how God built upon each component. As man build businesses, family, relationships, structures, and so forth, he too must carefully lay the correct foundation for it to sustain and last.

King Solomon was adamant about how to build them, He said:

"Prepare your work outside and make it ready for yourself in the field; afterwards build your house" **(Proverbs 24:27)**.

Most of the breaches in our family's foundation are because we did not properly prepare ourselves trans-generationally in the field (occupation); therefore, it will not yield enough sustenance and return to build a stable family life. This principle is totally opposite of how most people build their families. Notice the order I listed: business and then family. Many would argue that yo u build your family first, but that is not what Solomon stated.

Most modern-day families are started first and then the business or vocation. Maybe this practice is why our debt is so high and the divorce rate is over 50 percent? Most divorces are caused by failing to adhere to biblical principles regarding godly living, financial management, pre-marital co-habitation, pre-marital sex, no-marital sex, extra-marital sex, and disorder. Usually, the entire aforementioned means the family was built out of the order of God.

Day 5: Relationships

After four days God completed the foundation of heaven and earth, but there was no life form on earth. God filled the seas with great species and every kind of creature. He filled the air with every kind of winged species. He blessed them saying: "Be fruitful, multiply, and replenish the waters and the earth" (Genesis 1: 20-22). My Bible clearly states that He blessed them by speaking to the sea creatures and the birds; commanding them to be fruitful and multiply.

In essence, they were also commanded to "create" as well. He has provided all of the trees, plants, and herbs with seed yielding abilities for reproduction.

As you will notice, He did not put man first, why? There were no life-sustaining substance, and man or the other creatures could have survived without the sun, plants for food, or water. Planning is the importance of laying the correct systems in their order. When we believe by faith, many times we don't adhere to the system principles that warrant godly (Holy Spirit) intervention. The Holy Spirit will not get involved with your plans unless instructed by God. He will warn you and guide to all truths pertaining to plans that are not ordained by God.

I have done things that I knew were not approved by God. He warned me, but I forged ahead—only to fail in the end. The Holy Spirit is a Gentleman. He will not force himself on anyone, but He will definitely give you peace regarding decisions of complexity or expose the dangers of you moving forward with your plans. When we continue against His will, usually He sends another Christian to validate His desire for you not to continue with your plans. Lastly, if you listen to His Spirit, He will show you in His word what He has planned for you.

The Bible says: *"For God is not the author of confusion, but of peace, as in all churches of the saints"* (**1 Corinthians 14:33**).

The average man or woman becomes great only when they accomplish feats that seem impossible. The key ingredient is that they believed enough in the visions God presented to them and applied the basic principles of creativity to them. These principles and processes described previously contain keys necessary to unlock the mysteries of enhancing inventions, enhanced improvements, enhanced innovations, and futuristic dynamic benefits for mankind.

On the fifth day, God accomplished everything needed for man to begin occupancy and dominance on the earth.

We will carefully examine the sixth day, God's instructions to us. How He marveled and described all of his creation after the inclusion of man. Once we understand the inherent gift of faith, and accept that it grows based on our ability to trust God in what He has spoken and we walk in a level of hope and faith without considering failure as an option. His plan will then become instinctive and a dominant trait of our being. Adam and Eve experienced faith as a natural way of life until the great fall.

I emphasize these facts solely for reasons of stripping away your previous mindset in order to reintroduce you to your original place of beginning: a place of systems with God, a place of networks, a place relationship. A place of dominance, a place of glory, a place of nakedness, a place a natural beauty, a place of peace in nature, and a place of love to create anything God desires for you by faith and by works (Action).

Day 6: Relationships

According to the Book of Genesis; Moses wrote about the Six Day:

"Then God said, "Let the earth bring forth living creatures after their kind, cattle and creeping and the beast of the earth after their kind; and it was so. Then God said "Let Us make man in Our own image, and according to Our likeness and let them rule" **(Genesis 1:26).**

To summarize the remaining verses, God commanded Adam to rule over everything He created and to subdue it (Genesis 1:26-30). Afterwards, God saw all that He had made, and behold, it was described as **Very good"** And there was evening and there was the morning and the sixth day (Genesis 1:31). In the subsequent verses, Moses gives details of God's forming of man, saying:

"Then the Lord formed man of the dust from the ground and breathed into his nostrils the breath of life and man became a living creature" **(Genesis 2:7)**.

Let There Be Man and Woman!

"Then God said, "Let the earth bring forth living creatures after their kind, cattle and creeping and the beast of the earth after their kind; and it was so."

Then God said "Let us make man in our own image, and according to Our likeness and let them rule" **(Genesis 1:26)**.

God saw all that He had made, and behold, it was very good. And there was evening and there was morning, the six day **(Genesis 1:31)**.

The Lord God fashioned into a woman the rib which He had taken from the man, and brought her to man **(Genesis 2:22)**.

Please observe God's assessment of all that He had done and His view of man. He saw that it was all very good, when He included man. As we define "very" we are reminded of the marvelous thoughts which God has of us.

Webster defines *very* as in high degree; extremely; truly; absolutely; complete; absolute; being particularly suitable; being precisely as stated; genuine, true, and EXTRAORDINARY.

Now, what more can God say about us if we are made in His image? He completed the six days of creation with all things necessary for man to (1) create (2) to rule and (3) to subdue. In God's infinite wisdom, knowledge, and understanding, He omitted absolutely nothing from man's ability to excel and thrive in the transformation of earth into an oasis of enhanced inventions and innovations. Through the Holy Spirit, God will send His word to change and shift His earth to dispensations of modernization.

A Moment of Truth:***When God wants to change the earth, He does it through man!***

In God's divine infinite wisdom, knowledge, and understanding, He omitted absolutely nothing from man's ability to excel and thrive in the transformation of earth into an oasis of enhanced inventions and innovations. As stated earlier, we should tear down heaven's door for an assignment from Him. To have the opportunity to be in partnership with the Master of Creation is beyond excitement if we adopt this attitude.

The Bible says: *"God formed each animal out of the ground, He brought it to Adam to see what he would call them"* (**Genesis 2:19**).

He gave Adam complete control and dominance over each animal. God will bring you an assignment through revelation and inspiration to partner with you. It is always to dominate a territory, and He expects you to "Call it" and have dominion over it by using the measured gift of faith He placed in you for that vision. God created heaven and earth with words of truth and His evidence is still here today.

We should always speak the truth no matter what the consequences are. We must begin today, to build or rebuild our systems, networks and relationships solely on the foundation of truth in what God has said in His word. We must trust His principles and statutes and apply them in every area of our lives. Our words of truth must be living examples of what we *do* according to our faith in what God has shown us and by what we say will happen, will happen—according to His will. By always speaking the truth, I believe, it's the only way we can truly say to God, "Very good."

Chapter Seven
God's Day of Rest

In the summer of 2006, my eldest daughter Libby called me on my cell phone frantic, crying, and obviously in a state of panic and sheer terror. She had backed her car into a young man's vehicle while at an intersection, damaging the front of his hood.

After listening intently to her and calming her down; I said, "How are you darling, is anyone hurt?"

She answered, "No Dad, but I wrecked his car!"

My reply was one of the calm resolve of a loving father.

"Where are you sweet heart?"

Finally composing herself, she gave me her location, and

I said, "Don't sweat it; I'll be there in twenty minutes!"

"Be cool, relax and rest."

When I arrived at the scene of the accident, things had quieted. Everyone's temperament was restful, and both cars were stationed off the side of the road as if they were being prepped for a 12-point emissions team inspection. Pedestrians and motorists were rubbernecking to see what appeared to be no more than a minor fender-bender.

Also, the young man's parents had arrived with faces that represented the owners of the damaged portrait of Leonardo Di Vinci's, "Mona Lisa." After exchanging pleasantries with his parents and viewing the damage, it was obvious we would have to replace the damaged hood. Ironically, the young auto enthusiast drove an early 1980's model Chevy. I assured his parents we would restore the car to its original state as soon as possible.

The next morning Libby and I began calling auto parts shops in town, around town and out of town in search of a white hood to replace the damaged one. However, after talking to numerous dealers and to no avail, we discovered that finding an old Chevy hood that day might be a problem! We gave up our search after several hours and agreed to resume again the next day. We couldn't locate a hood of any color in Atlanta nor after an intense search on the Internet.

Finally, a friend informed me of a savage yard that might have that Chevy part in Griffin, Georgia. I contacted the owner, and he claimed to have several hoods for that model car as if he were: The Premier Antique Chevy Auto Parts Dealer of the South. I called Libby to tell her the good news and that I would come over in the morning to corral her to claim our precious treasure. She was extremely elated and relieved. I arrived very early the next day to pick up Libby and Paigie, (my youngest daughter) and we drove towards Griffin.

It was a beautiful morning as we listened to banging beats of rap music billowing out of my car speakers. We stopped for breakfast at a Huddle House restaurant on our way to Griffin to have breakfast where we were duly entertained by two local couples arguing over something that happened the previous night between the two husbands. Their argument eventually ensued into a scene reminiscent of a those infamously violent-feuds resembling the "Hatfield's and McCoy's."

It was a hilarious exchange of verbal assaults to each of their egos, and we all had a blast enjoying the ruckus. We finally got a chance to have breakfast and enjoy one another after the manager asked both parties to leave. I love to hear Libby and Paigie laughing together.

Oh, what a sound for a dad to enjoy! The laughter of two lovely daughter's in his ears... It's priceless! We were having a great time dining together and chatting about those men. We drank, ate, laughed, satisfied our hunger, tipped the waitress, and journeyed on. It was so nice being with the girls, driving and still laughing as we traveled down the back roads of South Georgia towards our destination.

We entered the parking lot in front of the main entrance of the Auto Parts Shop; we could barely see the rooftops of the collection of wrecked, abandoned and scavenged vehicles in that savage yard; because of the tall fence that obstructed our view. There were thousands of old cars of every make, model, color, and style behind that fortress, and we were aching to find our heralded prize. The shop door swung open as a young man stormed out with a smile as big as a Baby Grand Piano. He obviously found his part! We rushed inside and could see auto parts hanging from the ceiling, walls and behind the counter.

After talking with the owner, he directed us to the area where the older model Chevy's was. Surprisingly, as we walked through the property, I glanced to my left and there was a 1974 Mercury Capri, just like my first car I had purchased during my last year of High School.

My head swiveled around and around as if I were a giant hoot-owl perched on his nest in anticipation of an open feast of the variety of abundant prey. There was every type of car I had ever owned in that savage yard. Seeing those rusty and wrecked cars gave me an eerie feeling of shame, disgust, and disappointment.

Instantly, I remembered driving in similar cars and now there they were, symbolically retired, eulogized, and decomposing in the graveyard of the past. I thought about all the long nights, weekends, Sunday's, and extra hours I labored tirelessly to pay for those vehicles, and there they were, just like mines rusting, partially being picked-over by people for parts as bands-of-vultures devouring the carcasses' of dead animals. They all seemed so worthless and insignificant in comparison to my ex-wives, Libby, Paigie, and Fray Jr. I walked a little distance from them to reflect on what I had done to my family and to wipe away my tears. I didn't want them to see me crying. I could only say to myself, "What was I thinking about?" Were those cars worth all of the time I'd wasted away from my loved ones chasing after intangible materials? Now I realized how useless that time was spent.

I remembered how I just had to have those cars! The days, evenings, and nights that I missed being with my family and often away from so many of their important activities, it was all futile. I recalled being exhausted after working around the clock to complete some of my projects. Oftentimes, my body was still restless and in motion long after I was in bed. My body and my spirit constantly screamed for rest, but I was still driven to possess those worthless material possessions.

What a travesty? Sadly, it doesn't have to be a car. It could be a house, furniture, clothes, shoes, jewelry, boat, television, computer, cell phone, or whatever. It will eventually end up in somebody's salvage yard, backyard, jewelry box, garage, or garbage dump. What is so important that we risk our relationship with God and destroy or compromise our families and our health by not resting to acquire things that we can usually live without? What's even worse, I now don't possess any of those things that I sacrificed so many countless hours to have!

God has commanded us to rest our bodies as well as separate ourselves from the hustle and bustle of this demanding world. His desire is that we focus on Him and our families while He restores our spirits as well as our earthly vessels: our bodies. When we neglect to reserve a day of rest during the week with God, we are actually conveying our distrust and dishonor to our Creator as well ourselves. In the books of Genesis and Exodus, Moses describes God's activities or inactivity on the seventh day. Let's observe an extremely important command from God regarding the Sabbath day and its holiness.

He wrote: *"Remember the Sabbath day, to keep it holy. Six days you shall labor and do all your work"* **(Exodus 20:8-9)**.

Why would God tell us to "Remember the Sabbath day and keep it holy?"

Then God blessed the seventh day and sanctified it, because in it He rested from all of His work which God had created and made. This is the account of the heavens and earth when they were created, in the day that the Lord God made earth and heaven **(Genesis 2:3-4)**.

God has established a day of rest day for us to commune with Him in fellowship, intimacy, and blessings. If He said, "He blessed and sanctified the seventh day," why would we be laboring on that day?

Read the following passage carefully, please:

"For in six days the Lord made heaven and earth, and the seas, and all that in them is, and rested the seventh day: wherefore the Lord blessed the Sabbath day and hallowed it" (**Exodus 20:11**).

The word hallowed represents sacredness, holiness, sanctification, blessedness, consecration and deified. I just thought you should know that God has already promised to "Bless" that day in His word: "He blessed that day and sanctified it." Clearly stated, if we don't violate this command, He will have to honor our obedience. This day should be a day of happiness and rest. However, we do not trust that He will redeem any lost wages or what we perceive as opportunities. Instead, we proceed in justifying our many reasons as to why we have to continue and labor against His Word.

Jesus said in the Book of Matthew:

"Come to me all who are weary and heavy-laden and I will give you rest. "Take of my yoke upon me and learn from Me, for I am gentle and humble in heart, and YOU WILL FIND REST FOR YOUR SOULS. "For my yoke is and My burden is light" (**Matthew 11:28-30**).

I am not trying to force you into religion, legalism, or to live under the Law, but in the grand scheme of our plans for laboring on the Sabbath Day, we usually don't progress or benefit at all. When Christ came, He completely fulfilled the Law. There are numerous occasions where Jesus was questioned regarding the Sabbath. Paul, in his letter to the Romans explained the importance of living under grace when he wrote:

"One person regards one day above another, another regard every day alike. Each person must be fully convinced in his own mind. He who observes the day observes it for the Lord, and he who eats, does so for; for he gives thanks to God"

The grace and faith to live in Christ should compel us to trust God to rest our bodies, which are the temples where the Holy Spirit dwells at least one day a week. King David expressed it so eloquently in the Book of Psalms. He wrote:

"Unless the Lord builds the house, They labor in vain who build it; Unless the Lord guards the city, The watchman keeps awake in vain. It is vain for you to rise up early and retire late, to eat the bread of painful labors; for He gives to His beloved even in his sleep" **Psalms 127:1-2).**

Wow! Wow! "He gives to His beloved even his sleep."

Our nations are restless, exhausted, and desperately seeking solutions to the economic woes that grip our people. We are working tirelessly to balance the disparities in our lives, however, we are digressing more and more into a state of spiritual and physical poverty because we have ignored God's principles and continue to slip into the caverns of emotional, physical, and financial deficiency.

We will not work our way out of this mess without God. Until we recognize that our problems are spiritual, we will continue to work ourselves deeper into the doldrums of exhaustive efforts of disgrace. God can restore our nations, our spirits, our bodies, and our souls the moment we adhere to His commands... No other programs, stimulus packages, or campaigns will make a difference other than obedience to His word and to "Remember the Sabbath Day and keep it holy."

Chick-Fil-A: Corporate Sabbath

In case you have a problem believing God on a personal level. Let me give you a few corporate examples of companies that do not operate their businesses on Sunday. Samuel Truett Cathy, founder and Chairman of Chick-Fil-A Restaurants and Truett's Grill in Atlanta Georgia, does not open on Sundays, yet his companies are one of the fastest and most profitable growing chains in the world. As our generations change from the previous ones, to the Baby Boomers, Generation X, Y, Z, I and beyond so do their eating habits.

This metamorphosis has caused a major problem for the once popular chains, such as Mc Donald's, Burger King, Arby's, and Krystal causing closings of many of their restaurants around the world. These companies are opened seven days week and are having challenges with labor, growth, and profitability.

These problems were unheard of in previous years. Mr. Cathy has trusted and obeyed God's command, and his companies continue to grow and expand as one of the top Christian owned corporations in the world. I have taken the liberty to provide you with their Mission Statement from Chic-Fil-A. It reads:

"To glorify God by being a faithful steward of all that is entrusted to us and to have a positive influence on all who come in contact with Chick-Fil-A."

Lastly, a comment by a columnist: Some of you out west might have no idea what I'm talking about. My Church Marketing colleagues probably don't have a strong idea of what I'm talking about. But down South, it's about the Christian Chicken. Within 10 miles of my house, there are 10 Chick-Fil-A restaurants. One is open 24 hours a day.

Well, almost. It closes at 11:59 p.m. Saturday night and reopens at 5:00 a.m. Monday morning. It's a life style and an addition: chicken sandwiches, waffle fries, and sweet tea, that is. As you probably know, I'm a Christian. (Josh Cody, 2007-05).

Hobby Lobby

The next company I will feature is an Oklahoma based company called Hobby Lobby. It was founded by David Green in 1972. Early on Mr. Green made a conscience decision to close his stores on Sunday to give his employees time with their families and rest to enrich their lives. The stores are in 33 states and have expanded to a total of 403 locations. Mr. Green also believes that the use of expensive barcode systems commonly used by competitors would increase the cost of products so he decided to continue using standard registers for check out.

The music played in the stores is a collection of light jazz, classical, bluegrass, and contemporary styles with a blend of instrumental and traditional Christian hymns peacefully flowing over the speaker system throughout all of the stores continuously. Hobby Lobby locations have general operating hours from 9 a.m. to 8 p.m. Monday to Saturday except for the Distribution Center on certain days during the winter holiday season.

The mission statement for Hobby Lobby is:

Honoring the Lord in all we do by operating in a manner consistent with Biblical principles... Serving our employees and their families by establishing a work environment and company policies that build character, strengthen individuals, and nurture families. To provide a return on the owners' investment, and sharing the Lord's blessings with our employees, and invest in our communities.

God's command of us to rest on the seventh day is solely for the purpose of us to experience a spiritual regeneration and restoration of our spiritual and earthly vessels.

Historically, Sunday's were a day observed for God and our time with family. It was a day that families gathered to worship, eat together with friends, visit love ones, and yes, rest.

As we observed this day and all of its blessing, we are being set apart (sanctified) for an intimate and vital exchange of power, wisdom, knowledge, ideas, and under- standing, but most importantly to minister to God. I make it my point each week to take a day off. It does not have to be a particular day, just once a week. I get totally replenished and blessed as I rest.

Do you know the relationship King David had with God? God loves to hear praises unto Him. We should take this day and just express to God the beauty in what we see in the earth, the majesty and grandeur of His creation and His eternal (His love) beauty. We should tell Him about those six days that came out of His mind. Talk to Him about His Son (JESUS)! Praise Him for sending the Holy Spirit! Just expressing to Him how great He is w o u l d excite Him. We rarely minister to Him with the intent of just praise and thanksgiving. James, the Lord's (half- brother) elaborates in stating:

"Every good thing given and everything perfect gift is from above, coming down from the Father of lights, with whom there is no variation or shifting shadow" **(James 1:17)**.

God will continue to illuminate and bring clarity to His revelations as we dedicate ourselves to Him a day of rest and meditation on His word. We should call to His remembrance the Holy Scriptures He's written for us as we express the reverence and love we have for Him. We must take a day of rest to show honor and trust in knowing He will restore us and rejuvenate our spirits, bodies, and souls. It is impossible to spend intimate time with God and not be transformed and empowered.

We must be in hot pursuit toward the heart of God in hope of connecting our hearts with His. We must be synchronized with the same spiritual rhythm, with His will and plans for our families and lives in ministering to Him. David did not go to God in need only, but his going was to glorify and love on God with all of his heart.

In the 23rd Psalm David wrote:

"The LORD is my shepherd, I lack nothing. He makes me lie down in green pastures, he leads me beside quiet waters, He refreshes my soul. He guides me along the right paths for his name's sake. Even though I walk through the darkest valley, I will fear no evil, for you are with me; your rod and your staff they comfort me. You prepare a table before me in the presence of my enemies. You anoint my head with oil; my cup overflows. Surely your goodness and love will follow me all the days of my life, and I will dwell in the house of the LORD forever."

King David in his often fallen state purposed in his heart to have fellowship through a consistent pursuit of rest, intimacy and fellowship with God. Sometimes God has to make us lie down in the midst of our fears, doubts, and exhaustion to show us His goodness and mercy. Resting in God is powerful, yet simple, and unfortunately one of the major missing components to most of our spiritual failures. He prepares a place of peace and tranquility that overflows with His goodness and love.

Before King David anointed his son Solomon as the new king of Israel, he proclaimed the promise that God would give Solomon rest, quiet, and peace all the days of his life. Enclosing, I pray that you and your family will trust God and declare a day of **_rest_**, **_peace,_** and **_quiet_** in the presence of His glory and watch the very power of His love begin to over flow into every aspect of your lives. God said, "To remember that I have blessed and sanctified a Sabbath day and made it holy." So we might as well enjoy that day and rest in the Lord...

Chapter Eight
Faith in the Heart of Christ for Salvation

The journey that has brought me to this point is replete with what appeared to be disjointed episodes. Now I know that nothing is happenstance with God. We simply are not equipped to know or understand His ways. It is only now that I am able to begin to be able to connect the dots. One such episode in my life began on April 19, 1983, in Atlanta, Georgia. My best friend, Jeff Shingles and I had recently moved into our new office space

We were launching our new Telecommunications Company called, F.J. Communications. We were young businessmen excited and anxious to get our office established, decorated and open for business. Mr. James Galimore, a friend and former owner and office supply company would often drop in to ask if he could assist in any way and if we needed office supplies. We truly enjoyed Mr. Galimore visiting us. He was a man of wisdom and knew a great deal about business.

Frequently, he would invite us to his church, however, we were too busy trying to get the business off the ground, but would always decline until a later date. Mr. Galimore would often share his faith in Christ with us and his worship experiences nonetheless, he was always kind. I observed the obvious spiritual effect of his heart in his countenance. What I enjoyed most about him was he never harassed or badgered us about visiting his church, but continued to express his love for Christ and us. More importantly, he LIVED a life before us that was admirable.

We would spend enjoyable moments at the office just chatting about Christ. I wanted to know more about this faith after observing the evidence of Christ in this man's heart. So, I finally decided to take Mr. Galimore up on the offer and visit his church. I remember that Friday Evening Enrichment Service at the Fellowship of Faith International Church.

The music was great and there was a spirit of love in the air as we sang, "Its love, its love, its love that makes the world go round." We were hugging and greeting each other and I could feel the Spirit of God emanating out of the hearts of people and filling that sanctuary what appeared to be an eternity.

We sang many other songs as the band played instruments as if they were extensions of their bodies. They ministered in such great spiritual synchronization as the sounds from the piano, guitars, drums and the angelic voices of the singers were all on one accord producing a heavenly sound of praise. I had no doubt that this rich offering of praise ascended up directly into the presence of God. I had a blast trying to sing those songs I had never heard. I sang off-key and off-beat, but I didn't care for my heart was joyful as I sang just loud enough to drown out my missed words.

As the sound of the choirs music and peoples singing began to subside from its gradual-melodious-descent of what seemed like an extended spiritual journey, to a higher and loftier place than the earth's realm; there was such a peaceful feeling of liberty in the church that I knew could only come from God.

The praise and worship had been extremely engaging and ushered in the Spirit of God which prepared the hearts of the sincere worshipers for Pastor Wayne C. Thompson to begin his seemingly humble, but powerful message of faith. He talked about Jesus, faith, and the hope we have in salvation.

I had never heard a message that was so convincing that it compelled me to consider living that moment the rest of my life according to the Bible. I could feel the heart of Christ in that place, the love, the peace, the joy, the liberty, and the power that is only connected to the Spirit of God.

After his message, Pastor Wayne asked for those who didn't know Christ, but wanted to have a personal relationship with Him to come forward to the altar. I hesitated momentarily—pondering and visually panning the sanctuary for several minutes to see who was watching me. Anxiety kicked in, I could feel my heart racing but something inside urged me to take that proverbial stroll to the altar for salvation.

To this day I laugh at myself because I certainly enjoyed the service and the music. I also loved the message, which moved me to walk to the altar yet; I only made a *comment* to Christ, but not a *commitment*! My going to the altar that evening was not evidence of a repentant and contrite soul.

Moreover, my heart was not in that posture as of yet. I wanted to be at the right place spiritually, however, I still had a lot of growing to do. I had responded to a powerful message which touched me but my actions were no more than a ritualistic display of compassion for the humble pastor's sincere love for Christ and his ability to deliver a good sermon. I actually joined the church and became a member of the Fellowship of Faith International Church that evening as well. I attended the church for the next 10 years, but never really as an active member. I eventually left the church and for the next ten years I played "musical churches" until visiting New Birth Missionary Baptist Church in April 2004.

That evening my former wife accompanied me for Wednesday Night Bible Study. Before service started Bishop Long announced he was reducing the registration fee for an upcoming Men's Conference. My wife nudged me with her elbow and asked, "Are you going to attend!" I said, "I don't know." She reached into her purse and gave me twenty-five dollars and said, "You need to be here!" I had a pocket full of money, but took the offer.

I got up and walked out into the vestibule a n d registered for the conference. The following Friday, Dr. Tony Evans, from the Urban Alternative Ministry (Dallas, TX) was the guest speaker for the event. The title of his message was: *"Unless the Lord Builds the House They Labor In Vain Who Build It."* **(Psalm 127:1).**

His message convicted me to the core of my being. I walked out of the sanctuary that evening completely a changed person, and on my way to my car I made a total commitment to live the rest of my life serving Christ. I stood next to this huge boulder in the rear of the Church and said, "Lord, I know I am not living the way you would have me live, this day, I give my all to you. I commit my total heart... Do whatever you want with me."

Please note this was ten years after the earlier walk to the altar where, I admit, my intent was good however my commitment was shallow.

I returned home that evening and told my wife what had happened. We put the kids to bed after prayer, I said to her:

"I would like to talk with you."

She said, "Okay!"

I had bought her two books and asked Dr. Evans to autograph them for her. He was her favorite! I said: "The Lord is not the center of our marriage, our home or our business." She begged to differ, but I felt He wasn't. I expressed to her that I made a personal commitment to serve God the rest of my life. That decision in April 2004 would change my household forever. Serious trouble began. My thinking and allegiance began to change. Some of my actions were misinterpreted. Bigtime!

Weeks later we had a terrible argument beginning with a baseless accusation that I was involved in an affair with an old friend. The tension escalated. After several weeks of arguing the accusation of infidelity levied against me became so disruptive that it forced me to vacate the premises and my home. The accusation was totally unfounded and untrue. There was nothing I could say to convince my wife or prove my innocence. Even though some statistics claim that 55% of all married persons are unfaithful, I had managed to remain true to my wife. Any suggestion otherwise initially hurt and later infuriated me. During that period my youngest kids were visiting their grandparents in New Jersey; they would never come home to their mother and father as a couple again. I was devastated. This kind of trouble either drives one to destruction or straight to God. I chose the latter!

I arrived at my office that afternoon determined to have a renewed and deeper relationship with God. I entered the conference room depleted and in a state of disgust, I fell to my knees and told God I was tired of the arguments and the disunity. I wanted to truly know Him at another level—a level that would allow me to get through this trial. I needed a faith transfusion! I couldn't fathom the thought of permanently losing my wife nor did I anticipate the harsh reality of another failed marriage. I was assured that after a few days' things would settle down after my wife's anger dissipated. I lay on the floor of my conference room in sheer pain and began praying in search for a word of comfort.

I opened my Bible to the first chapter of the Gospel of John, by accident (or so I thought). I began reading:

In the beginning was the Word, and the Word was with God, and the Word was God. He was in the beginning with God. All things came into being through Him, and apart from Him nothing came into being that has come into being. In Him was life, and the life was the Light of men. The Light shines in the darkness, and the darkness did not comprehend it. There came a man sent from God, whose name was John. He came as a witness, to testify about the Light, so that all might believe through him. He was not the Light, but he came *to testify about the Light. There was the true Light which, coming into the world, enlightens every man. He was in the world, and the world was made through Him, and the world did not know Him. He came to His own, and those who were His own did not receive Him. But as many as received Him, to them He gave the right to become children of God, even to those who believe in His name, who were born, not of blood nor of the will of the flesh nor of the will of man, but of God* **(John 1-13)**.

And then I read verse fourteen:

"And the Word became flesh, and dwelt amongst us, and we saw His glory, glory as the only begotten from the Father, full of grace and truth" **(John 1:1-14)**.

I read that verse again, again, again and again—until the light of Christ was so bright that His presence was in that room. I lay on the floor with my face toward the carpet because I was so embarrassed, I felt ashamed, because in spite of earlier claims and attempts, I had not really known Jesus until that day. I thought the Word was the Bible (because I never really studied). After all of those years of listening to ministers on the radio and watching televangelist—I did not know the Word was Jesus. That was the day I saw His glory and fully committed my whole heart. It was my "Damascus Road" experience. I fully acknowledged Him that moment as: **Jesus, the Son of God!**

You will never have that revelatory moment in Christ until your heart is completely open and you 'cry-out' to Him for a true and full encounter, where you totally *see* Him as the Son of God and *believe* with all of your heart. I share my story because as I look at the matter in hindsight, I now realize that I experienced Jesus in a series of encounters, each more profound than the one before. It took a while but I finally came to know Him in the fullest.

Regretfully, in spite of my desire to keep my home intact my marriage was not healed. For the responsibility and duties as the priests of our home were yet my assignment, I did not cover, protect or have compassion for her or my family during that experience because of the hardness of my heart. I should have known better. Now I realize that when Christ calls a married couple (as I believe was the case in our marriage) it can introduce and even more delicate, sensitive number of challenges, as it did in my marriage.

I Then entered another regretful phase of my journey— that of bitterness and reactionary behavior. In retrospect, I can truly confess, I did not manage the separation from my wife and family with a forgiving and repentant heart. My heart became hardened toward her for accusing me of infidelity and my being kept away from my kids.

I believe if I had continued exhibiting godly love and not had an unforgiving heart with bitterness included; we may have reconciled. Oftentimes, a spouse does not understand or agree with what their loved one is hearing for fear their life will become drastically altered with the confusion of the 'called' (God is not the Author of confusion. We are when we don't submit to His will) trying to maneuver through the spiritual fog and the commitment to living a Christian life.

I have personally experienced and witnessed couples struggle with the transformation of this experience. I cannot answer why God's call affects some couples often adversely... while others favorably; other than what Jesus says in His word. In the Book of Matthew, He wrote:

"Do not think that I came to bring peace on earth. I did not come to bring peace but as word For I have come to 'set a man against his father, a daughter against her mother, and a daughter-in-law against her mother-in-law' "and 'a man's enemies will be those of his own household" **(Matthew 10:34-36).**

Our hearts must be committed to Christ, our families and the ones we say we love and not become bitter, but we must allow the Holy Spirit to change our heart (not theirs) as we pursue Christ and continue to love those who we feel persecute us. In addition, I listened to some ill-advised counseling from people who meant well, but were not qualified in areas of marriage.

Important truth: ***Never seek advice from a single person who has never been married about certain aspects of your marriage.***

They ***may not*** properly advise or guide you. Jesus spoke about why our marriages often fail. In the book of Matthew, as He was being questioned and tested by the Pharisees regarding divorcing their wives:

"He said to them, Because of the hardness of heart Moses permitted you to divorce your wives; but from the beginning it has not been this way. And I say to you, whoever divorces his wife except for immorality, and marries another woman commits adultery" **(Matthew 19:8-9).**

I was cautioned by an elder from my church of the consequences of divorce, but I felt it was justified by the negative actions of my wife. However, my reaction has subsequently cost my family and me enormous pain and loss. The hardness of people's hearts has caused many individuals to make decisions that have ended their marriages prematurely. We truly don't consider the adverse trans-generational effect we call into motion because we refuse to examine the deeper ramifications of an uncommitted heart for Christ and our families.

Whether you are called to full time ministry or whether you are simply called to serve and witness for Christ, there are certain measures and other factors which should be considered prior to making what should be a lifetime selection. Choosing your mate (husband or wife) is one of the most important decisions you will ever make in life: do not take this selection lightly.

The wrong choice in a mate can spell disaster, loss of dreams, loss of purpose, loss of time, loss of liberty, and possibly loss of life.

The two of you must love God more than each other. Both must place Him at the epicenter of your marriage. He must be invited as the Mediator in all conflicts and agreements based on the word of God. Equally important, is that you have comparable levels of belief and faith and live by the standards set forth in the Bible. I have no desire or intent to blame either of the two women that I married for the breakup of the relationship.

I have already accepted full blame for the failure of them. I did not heed to the advice I have just given you. I *quit* before allowing God to workout the proper solution or finish the process He had me going through.

The importance of a godly foundation was not at the center of my criteria. It was more about me, my feelings and physical desire. The success and the legacy of your family are dependent upon the cohesiveness and unity of the husband and wife if you are married. When there is constant discord and disharmony, the trans-generational concept is at risk.

A marriage's fate MUST be targeted with faith, hope, and the greatest of all, LOVE as the foundation for its existence. Any other concept will be destructive, self-serving, self-centered, and constant struggle. Today our society is so quick to shift from a true commitment in Christ and marriage when their *perception* turns into *persecution* from those we love as we follow Him. Didn't Jesus distinctly say, "You shall suffer persecution because of Me?" Ironically, we must understand that the entire relationship with Christ is based on a marriage? Paul wrote how love is to be demonstrated by husbands towards their wives in his letter to the Ephesians stating:

"Husbands, love your wives, just as Christ also loved the church and gave Himself up for her, so that He might sanctify her, having cleansed her by the washing of water with the word, that He might present to Himself the church in all her glory, having no spot or wrinkle or any such thing; but that she would be holy and blameless" **(Ephesians 5:25-27).**

Faith and love should factor greatly in selecting a mate; consequently living in harmony based on God's Words...

Did I love my former wife as Christ loved the Church? No!
Did I give myself up for her? No!
Did I allow Christ to sanctify her? No!
Did I blame her? Yes!
Did I counsel and lead my former wife with the Word? No!
Did I allow Christ to change my heart? No!
Did I pray and wait for Christ to change her heart? No!
Did I follow the instructions that were in the Bible? No!
Did I resort to my feelings and allow my hardened heart to dictate my actions? Yes! I did not apply the principles of Faith in the Bible. I did not allow the Word to work.

Paul gave his opinion on how a married couple should behave in 1 Corinthians Chapter 7, He wrote:

"To the rest I say this (I, not the Lord): If any brother has a wife who is not a believer and she is willing to live with him, he must not divorce her. And if a woman has a husband who is not a believer and he is willing to live with her, she must not divorce him. For the unbelieving husband has been sanctified through his wife, and the unbelieving wife has been sanctified through her believing husband. Otherwise your children would be unclean, but as it is, they are holy. But if the unbeliever leaves, let it be so. The brother or the sister is not bound in such circumstances; God has called us to live in peace. How do you know, wife, whether you will save your husband? Or, how do you know, husband, whether you will save your wife?" (Verses: 12-16).

Divorce is a very delicate reality that I believe the Church has not properly addressed. I have heard pastors dance around this subject and leave divorced members confused and hopeless. The church and its leaders often treat divorce as the unpardonable sin, even classifying it above other sins (murder and etc...) more heinous in nature.

Many Christians live in condemnation for years because of divorce and oftentimes. suffer through numerous and sometimes dangerous circumstances far beyond their control. Every day people walk out of their marriages leaving their believing spouse broken hearted and in a state of confusion and pain.

All the praying in the world won't change an individual's heart if he or she is determined to seek what they consider is freedom. A lady whose husband decided he did not want to be married to her anymore, called her after a few years and said, "I miss you, I will always love you and I just wanted you to know!" She said, "You are where you want to be and with whom you want to be with" (S. Butler).

Granted, there are certain conditions (abuse, infidelity or violence) when one should end a marriage. However, I highly recommend prayer, counseling and professional intervention to help transition you through this period of extreme, physical and emotionally challenging times; if divorce is imminent. When a marriage fails, God gives us the grace and peace to pick up the pieces and move forward. He doesn't want you wallowing in self-pity and self- condemnation for years.

God's love delivers us from the bondage of perceived personal failure and spiritual brokenness. He will give you a new life and a new hope as He becomes your new spouse until He gives you the peace, joy and grace to possibly love (marry to a believer) again, if it's His will. Again, it is a matter of faith in God to heal the brokenness and restore your spirit to love and trust again. Faith, the gift of salvation, the heart of Christ and our marriages are uniquely interconnected spiritually and should never be divided.

Once we integrate Christ into the heart of our relationship and marriage, He becomes the final mediator and regulator to guide and direct our steps for a complete union of love and harmony, which cements Him as the foundation of our salvation and creates an unbreakable bond and a endless marriage.

A Matter of Relationship

The hearts have it! Amazingly enough, King David's love for God was in his heart. His father (Jesse) wanted to choose Eliab his older brother because of his statue and good looks to be king. However, God chose David because of his heart and made him king over all His people. What do you think He will do for you? Aren't you also capable of having a heart which loves God and His people? Aren't you capable of exhibiting genuine faith? David was anointed king because he believed (displayed FAITH) and loved God with all of his heart. His love was displayed constantly as he combined poetry, praise and dance as indicated in many of his writings. The Book of Psalms contains numerous revelations from David.

"The Lord said to my Lord, "Sit at the place of honor at my right hand until I humble your enemies, making them a footstool under your feet" **(Psalm 110:1).**

David's faith allowed him to develop an intimate relationship with God through believing with his heart and confessing his love for Him in poetry, song, dance and praise. His life was so impacted by that same faith, he often played musical instruments and would dance in praise to God. His faith granted him unprecedented access into the presence of His Glory.

Likewise, our faith in Christ starts with salvation and a personal relationship with the Author and Finisher of our faith.

This is why a time of worship and praise should be paramount in our encounters with God. The relationships we have established on earth with men should be microcosms in comparison to our relationship with Christ. He opened, closed and locked the doors of hell and validated our entry key to heaven forever. The very act of His death gives us eternal access to the once closed gates of heaven.

Again, Paul invited believers to, "Come boldly to the throne of grace in time of help and need." Allow me to share a piece of advice which I realized only after many years on this journey. Please remember and take it seriously. This is a priceless nugget of truth: *The greater the relationship with Christ the greater access you will have to Him...*

In my earthly relationships there are certain people I trust with certain levels of closeness or proximity. My children for example, have relatively full access at any time they choose. In contrast, others have only limited access during restricted times. It's all a matter of relationship, personal safety, spiritual protection and purpose. An intimate relationship with Christ is indeed a safe one. You can be as transparent with Him as possible and never have to worry about being betrayed, berated or degraded.

I am **excited** that you have or will acknowledge Him as the Son of God! This is paramount and the most important relationship in your life. The moment you believe that He is the Christ, as He blessed Peter, He will also bless you and me. Jesus freed you and I from every form of bondage, fear, torment, oppression, brokenness, addiction; and every form of poverty was taking away at the Cross.

The apostle Paul makes it plain and simple. He stated: *"Brethrens, my heart desire and prayer to God for Israel is that they might be saved"* (Romans 10:1).

Faith VS Doubt = An Unsettled and Unfulfilled Spirit

If we can ever harness the tiny amount of faith it takes to operate in the Kingdom of Heaven spirit we will then experience the earthly manifestation of equivalent greatness. Jesus told the disciples:

"Truly I say to you, among those born of woman there has not risen anyone greater than John the Baptist! Yet the one who is least in the kingdom of heaven is greater than he. "From the days of John the Baptist until now the Kingdom of Heaven suffers violence and violent men take it by force" **(Matthew 11:11-12).**

History reveals that most often a takeover of any kingdom, doctrine, philosophy, religion, and government or belief system involves the presence or use of violence. It is not uncommon for the process to reveal ravage, carnage and death, sometimes to a massive extent. The violence Jesus speaks of can only be that of a *spiritual* and not *physical* state.

As kingdom alignment and privilege becomes a part of an individual's existence, one can anticipate a violent spiritual death of the existing life to the birthing of another. If able to conceptualize and describe the actual birthing process, a newborn would probably share that the journey is dark, full of pressure and will most often include a rather violent "slap" upon arrival! What a way to enter the world! What a way to be born!

The New Birth

That is why Jesus told Nicodemus, "Truly, Truly, I say to you, **unless one is born again he cannot see the kingdom of God**" (John 3:3, bold emphasis mine).

We are just like Nicodemus, who could not conceive the thought of Jesus' statement and asked, "How can a man be born when he is old? He cannot enter a second time into his mother's womb and be born again, can he?"

Jesus answered, "**Truly, truly, unless one is born of the water and of the Spirit he cannot enter into the kingdom of God. That which is born of the flesh is flesh and that which is born of the Spirit is spirit**" (John 3:5, bold emphasis mine).

Undoubtedly, once we believe that Jesus is "The Christ" and truly have an intimate spirit-filled encounter with Him, which will lock away our old mindset forever; then and only then will He give us the **keys** to the kingdom of heaven. Our relationship with Him requires that we reject our carnal way of reason and emulate every authentic word and image we read and comprehend about Christ. He told Peter "keys," denoting multiple doors of entry to power, glory, majesty and dominion.

What prevents us from unlocking and gaining permanent access to the kingdom of heaven is the *passive* attitude we have of Christ: "**For the kingdom of God is not eating and drinking, but righteousness and peace and joy in the Spirit**" (Romans 14:17).

Our image of Christ is so distorted that for centuries we have passed it (thinking) down from one generation to the next.

We must become spiritually violent by forcing our way in... by believing in Him without doubt, unprecedented since that day at Calvary. Then we will say: "Truly, He is the Christ!"

Jesus taught a favorite New Testament lesson on "Attitudes" to His disciples that should encourage those who desire to follow Him even in the midst of discomfort, misunderstanding and violence which may find its way into their lives on the journey. He stated:

Blessed are the poor in spirit for theirs is the kingdom of heaven

Blessed are those who mourn for they shall be comforted

Blessed are the gentle for they shall inherit the earth

Blessed are those who hunger and thirst after righteousness, for they shall be satisfied.

Blessed are the merciful for they received mercy

Blessed are the pure in heart for they shall see God

Blessed are the peacemakers, for they shall be called the sons of God

Blessed are those who have been persecuted for righteousness for theirs is the kingdom of heaven

Blessed are you when people insult you and persecute you, and falsely say all kinds of evil against you because of me. "Rejoice and be glad, for your reward in heaven is great; for in the same way they persecuted the prophets who were before you" **(Matthew 5:3-12).**

At the time Jesus was teaching His leaders (disciples) to rejoice and be happy in the mist of persecution and challenges. In the midst of unrest and trouble He brings comfort.

No man or woman without the power of God (Holy Spirit) residing in them could tolerate being persecuted and reviled constantly without heavenly powers. The power within a person is not revealed in how much he or she retaliates, but their willingness to restrain themselves and effectively love another in opposition. Jesus came with demonstrations of power and authority. The Book of Matthew is replete with examples of His power in manifestation.

In the fourth chapter we find this account:

Jesus was going throughout all of Galilee, teaching and proclaiming the gospel of the kingdom, and healing every kind of disease and every kind of sickness among the people. The news about Him spread throughout all Syria; and they brought to Him all who was ill, those suffering with various diseases and pains, demoniacs, epileptic, paralytics; and He healed them. Large crowds followed Him from Galilee and the Decapolis and Jerusalem and Judea and from beyond the Jordan (**Matthew 4:23-25**).

Christians have presented diluted or watered-down teaching in this area. For three and one-half years the people were fully assured that if Jesus appeared in their presence that **all** of their afflictions would be solved. Although it is the most powerful institution in the universe, the kingdom of heaven often depicted as small in origin, but with overwhelming power and exponential growth after the philosophy, principles and action are applied.

I must elaborate further before introducing you to salvation and provide you with mounting evidence that should incite you to want to enter into this privilege of inherited kingdom of heaven power unlike you have ever seen.

Once you receive the keys by faith, there is no limit to what you can do on earth. It is literally giving you power equal or greater than what Jesus displayed during His earthly visitation. He actually stated, "And greater things shall you do!" Jesus often spoke in parables, (short stories) He could not explain the kingdom of heaven principles to people because their *mindset* required a total, violent, forceful and mental shifting from everything they had experienced or heard. It will require the same from you and me as well. Jesus came as a representative demonstrating its power, attributes and deity. That is why he said, "Repent for the Kingdom of Heaven is at hand!" He did not say, repent for Jesus is here! No, He did not say that!!

We have mistakenly misused the word "repent" which means: to turn from the **_wrong_** direction you have been going and get back on **_the righteous_** track of following Christ. We are charged to move into the kingdom of heaven and all of its attributes, power and as a result "**Be**" them. This statement is in no way meant to remove the Mediator (Christ) from the equation; He stands between you and this experience.

You must go through Him to get the full benefits, glory and power, there is no other way! If it were necessary for Him to be here for us to exercise these rights, He would have remained with us in the physical realm. Instead, He gave us full use of it and even more before returning to His Father in Heaven.

Before His departure He said:

"Truly, truly, I say to you, he who believes in Me, the works that I do he will do also; and greater works than these he will do, because I go to the Father. Whatever you ask in my name, I will do it. If you love Me you will keep my commandments" (John 14:12-15).

Salvation Is Yours

It is my prayer that one day we (the Church) will get the 'salvation thing' right. For too long it has been little more than a benign ritual. Remember the earlier walk I made to the altar. It was only an external statement without internal commitment. Traditionally, salvation has not been introduced with power and wonders nor with the great expectations of what's to follow. I purposed to approach this awesome privilege with zeal and excitement, so that it will have a far greater significance for you from this moment and in the future come.

For those whom have experienced salvation and not the kingdom of heaven, I pray that you ask Jesus as He stated, for the "Violence" to forcefully enter into the kingdom of heaven and begin operating (being) in the many powers that are at your disposal. Now, if you are reading this and you are not saved, please let's take care of this now! Because my heart's desire is that YOU might be saved! If you are not saved this is your greatest moment! I said, 'this is your greatest moment!'

The apostle Paul loved Israel and the Gentiles so much that he preached salvation through Christ with emphasis by faith, so I will as well. He wrote:

"How then can they call on him to save them unless they believe in him? And how can they believe in him if they never heard about him? And how can they hear about him unless someone tells them? And how will anyone go and tell them without being sent? That is why the Scripture say, "How beautiful are the feet of messengers who bring good news!" But not everyone welcomes the Good News, for Isaiah the prophet said, "Lord, who has believed our message?" So faith comes from hearing, that is, hearing the Good News about Christ." **(Romans 10:14-17).**

A Moment of Redemption!

"But what say it? The word is near you and in your mouth and in your heart, which is the word of faith, which we preach. That if you shall confess with your mouth the Lord Jesus, and shall believe in your heart that God raise Him from the dead you shall be saved"
(Romans 10:8-9).

You are now ready to enter into a new realm of existence—one with full privilege, promise and power! It is a simple matter. Just open your mouth and speak the following: Declare these words:

I, _____ confess with my mouth the Lord Jesus, and believe with my heart that God raised Him from the dead and that Jesus Christ is the Son of God!! For it is by believing in your heart that you are made right with God. And it is by confessing with your mouth that you are saved.

If you have walked away from the Church and your commitment to Christ, let's repent, recommit, and refresh ourselves to a better way of life in Him. If you were not saved and you declared these words, I welcome you to the household of faith through Jesus Christ! Amen, Amen, and Amen!

Now that you have taken care of your salvation, if you do not have a church home, pray and ask God to guide you to the place of worship, He would have you to grow and mature in. The heart is what God wants! He wants us to be like sponges and our hearts to absorb all of His. Even if you have been betrayed or let down before, you have just connected with a heart that is flawless—AND FAITHFUL!

The Bible tells us to, "Guard your heart with all diligence for out of it flows the issues of life." If our hearts are in the same stream with God then we become godly tributaries emanating righteous issues that are constantly flowing from Him to us. Jesus also said, "Out of the abundance of the heart the mouth speaks" (Matthew 12:34). That abundance Jesus spoke of is based on the condition of our hearts, if we have godly thoughts and holiness inside of us that is what will flow from us. Then there is the matter of the Holy Spirit, a heavenly power Jesus sent after His departure. His presence in our lives brings clarity explained and special connection.

The Bible says, Jesus began preparing the disciples for His Calvary experience, ultimate ascension back to His Father in heaven. He explained to them the fate of events to come and what to expect. Hearing of His impending death was obviously perplexing as they began grieving because of the disturbing news. Jesus had spoken subtly through parables and stories concerning the kingdom of heaven and His eventual return; they just refused to believe Him. However, He promised that He would not leave them without an advocate; that He would send a Comforter the (Holy Spirit).

He expressed to the disciples the many benefits of Him leaving and how the world has already been judged by His death. He expounded deeper into how the Holy Spirit will only do what He is commanded to do. Jesus explained His *relationship* with the Holy Spirit and how He would reveal to them things that would happen in the future. He wanted them to understand that they were getting a Helper equal to Himself, but with greater power. Nonetheless, the disciples were mourning in spite of the promise of a greater exchange. They could not fathom or believe what they were hearing from Jesus.

Today we have the same problem receiving the Holy Spirit. In spite of all the facts and His indisputable evidence in existence we still question His presence. We are experiencing His divine power on a daily basis and don't recognize the insurmountable proof of His grace in their lives even though we see the signs, wonders, and revelation. Even scientists and great scholars are hard pressed to dismiss certain incidents (phenomenal events, healings, miracles, and etc...) as mere coincidence.

The Holy Spirit demonstrates the power and attributes of what we read in the Bible, by His ever-presence and action in our lives. He is the proven evidence that what Jesus promised to the disciples He was able to do—as He returned and resumed His rightful place with His Father in heaven praying for us.

Chapter Nine
Faith to Pray to Receive the Baptism in the Holy Spirit
(The Power of God)

Unless you have experienced the baptism in Holy Spirit, it is very difficult to understand what is meant by this heavenly event. My experience is one of dire humility, honor, and grace. All of my reading and shouting could not have prepare me for what I was about to encounter that morning in apartment 808. I do not know why God chose that day to impart His Holy Spirit upon me. He is certainly not something I deserved or could ever deserve. I still have not operated in the fullness of His divine Gift to this day. Years ago, I had lunch with Pastor Wayne Thompson, and he asked,

"Have you received the Holy Spirit?"

"I said, No!" He said,

"You will not have the power **_you will need_** to do ministry without the Baptism of the Holy Spirit."

I did not understand then, but I do know now what pastor Wayne meant by that statement. I was finally baptized in the Holy Spirit in the spring of April 2007.

I was introduced to Wayne Dowtin at a high school basketball game by William Cameron, my good friend.

After meeting Wayne, he seemed overzealous in his love for Christ. I thought to myself, 'This guy is cocky and arrogant. He can't love Christ that much.' I had never met anyone so excited about Christ. I never said a word to William about my feelings until after I received the Holy Spirit.

However, several months later we attended a special meeting for the Men's Ministry on a Thursday evening. Surprisingly, Wayne attended. He wasn't a member of our church, so I was shocked when I saw him there. We exchanged pleasantries, hugged, and took our seats. After our meeting, several of the brothers congregated outside the church to pray for a fellow brother who was having marital and domestic issues to pray for him and his family. We all completely surrounded him and began to pray.

After we finished praying for our brother, Wayne said to me, "Man, I pray every morning at seven o'clock. Would you like to pray with me Fray?" He spoke to me only. I did not want too, but he prodded and asked me again. "Fray would like to pray with me?" I begrudgingly said, "Sure!" I gave him my business card and journeyed home. My former wife had been calling (we were separated at that time) me all day and night up until midnight. I refused to answer the phone because we had been unkind to one another the day before. Friday morning around 6:45... she called again. That time I answered. She had been trying to tell me our dog Nikki (our Irish Setter) was dying, and I should come to see her before the veterinarian puts her down.

I had no idea that Nikki was even sick. She told me they had to put her to sleep last night. As I was talking with her, Wayne called me on my cell phone. I was so distraught and traumatized; I had completely forgotten about him calling. His first call went to voice mail. As I continued with my wife, "I told her I would come to the house in 20 minutes."

As soon as I hung up from her, Wayne called again. I did not recognize his number because he had never called me before. I was troubled, dejected, and flustered.

I said, "Hello!"

He said, "Fray this is Wayne!" "Good Morning, are you ready to pray?"

I said "Wayne, I can't talk right now. I've got to go!"

He said, "What's wrong?"

I replied, "I've got to go!" "My life is a mess."

"I'm separated, my marriage is jacked up, my business is bad, my dog just died and I don't know what to do."

"Let's pray," Wayne persisted.

I said, "I've got to go to my house."

Wayne said, "Wait!" "What do you want to tell God?"

"I don't know." I replied!

Again, he asked, "What do you want to tell God?"

"I don't know man, my life is a mess."

I got on my knees with the cell phone in my left hand and my face buried in my couch. Wayne began praying. He prayed for my wife, my family, my marriage, my business, and for the joy we had with Nikki. "You were blessed going into your business; you are blessed coming out of it."

I stood up, began walking around my living room with my eyes closed. I paced around, around and around... He continued praying and quoting God's word to me. Wayne was praying Scriptures that were colliding, exploding and penetrating my heart in truth because I knew them. Each time Wayne prayed a Bible verse, I would say:

"I hear you, Lord!"

"I hear You, Lord!"

"I hear You, Lord!"

"I hear You, Lord!"

"I hear You, Lord!"

And on my sixth, "I hear you, Lord," I felt this mighty-rushing-wind enter into my apartment and knock me off of my feet. I still had that cell phone in my left hand as I lay on my back crying and trembling. I began speaking a foreign language, telling Wayne, "I just received the Holy Spirit with the evidence of speaking in tongues." What I believed happened was my heart agreed with the Word of God as Wayne prayed, I had complete confidence in God to make things right. I believed with my heart through Wayne's prayer that we had established a direct connection to the Throne of Grace; and God had sent the Holy Spirit to baptize me with His power and fulfill His promise to comfort me.

What I did not know was that Wayne has an intense prayer life, but he knew by his faith and his relationship with Christ that God was able to help me in my time of need. I also learned that you never speak ill of anyone's love, actions for Christ or of anyone else in general. We are all God's children and no one has the right to criticize anyone.

It was one of the most humbling experiences of my life in judging God's people. I had prayed numerous times in other settings to receive the Holy Spirit, but it is not a gift you can just dial up and order. It is a heart experience that only God can give through obedience and belief in His Word. I do realize after receiving the Holy Spirit that it is preceded by sincere and earnest communion with God.

My experience is similar to the Scripture in the Book of Acts. Luke wrote:

"These all with one mind were continually devoting themselves to prayer, alone with the woman, and Mary the mother of Jesus, and with His brothers" (**Acts 1:14**).

Prayer seems to be the mechanism that petitions God to send us His Holy Gift. According to the Book of Acts, Jesus told the apostles not to leave Jerusalem, but to wait for Him to send the Holy Spirit.

Who is the Holy Spirit?

He is the Third Person of the Trinity: God the Father, God the Son (Jesus), and God the Holy Spirit.

In essence, He is God invisible on earth.

In this chapter, I will by the grace of God, the intercession of Jesus Christ and the leading of His Spirit give my very best effort to present the Holy Spirit to you with simplicity, truth, and the power of His God ordained omnipresent, omnipotent, and omniscience powers.

The *word Omni* means: All.

He's ALL Present!
He's ALL Potent!
He's ALL Science!

In essence, He's the All in All!

According to Paul in his epistle to the Ephesians:

"There is one body and one Spirit, just as you were called to one hope when you were called; one Lord, one faith, one baptism; one God and Father of all, who is over all and through all and in all" **(Ephesians 4:4-6).**

The word *Present* means: current, contemporary, be there, incidence, existence, and occurrence. The word *Potent* means: powerful, strong, effective, forceful, compelling, persuasive, intoxicating, and heady. The word *Science* means: discipline, knowledge, skill, art, learning, and scholarship. I could stop here but you still might not believe.

We have not advanced much in the last two-thousand plus years in understanding and respecting this most unique member of the Godhead. Unfortunately, our ineffective lives are representations of how we truly believe in the Holy Spirit and His God delegated powers and authority.

The word *Holy* is to most people such a mysterious connotation to the point that we have totally reduced the Holy Spirit to some scary, ghostly being that has little to no relevance or existence other than being spooky! He is the **only** member of the **Godhead** that must be reverenced and never spoken ill of, NEVER! Jesus warned us of the eternal dire-consequence of such and unpardonable offence. He said:

"Therefore I say to you, every sin and blasphemy will be forgiven men, but the blasphemy against the Spirit will not be forgiven men. Anyone who speaks a word against the Son of Man, it will be forgiven him; but whoever speaks against the Holy Spirit, it will not be forgiven him, either in this age or in the age to come" **(Matthew 12:31-32).**

Webster defines *holy* as consecrated, blessed, sacred, divine, righteous, hallowed, and sanctified. Currently, as a church body, we have very little evidence and understanding of the godly attributes that make up His divine character. God gave explicit orders. He said, "Be ye holy for I am Holy" (meaning without sin). The word *spirit* is life-force, soul and mind.

The first mention of the Holy Spirit is recorded in the first chapter of Genesis. Moses' describes Him as an active, obedient and participating member in creating the heavens and the earth; by the instructions and empowering of God. Moses wrote, "And the Spirit of the God was moving upon the face of the deep, and God said, "Let there be light," and there was light (Genesis 1:2).

The thought of me conceptualizing the infinite power and characteristics of God's Spirit would be worthless, futile and a theoretical attempt to describe the indescribable. Just as the 120 Christians waited for Him in the upper room in Jerusalem, they did not know what to expect because He had not shown Himself before.

God's desire is that we view Him as unlimited and all-possible Supreme Being who is eagerly waiting for us to ask Him to demonstrate more of Himself through us. As I write this statement, I realize we are guilty of binding God and the Holy Spirit from doing marvelous works in our lives because we don't know Him. Our disobedience, disbelief, fears, and lack of trust prevent Him from doing the impossible through us, thereby making Him archaic, powerless in our minds, and dormant because we dare to believe beyond our historical accomplishments and continue to live on the reputation of our former, private and public accolades.

Notice the event in Genesis: The Bible says. He was "moving" (participating) and was listening for a command. And God said: "Let there be light." He created light by the delegated power of God (obedience). Now, let's agree that the Holy Spirit fully participated and was absolutely obedient to the commandment and power of God.

It was a simple exhibition of God delegating His Holy Power to His Holy Spirit to do His divine work. This way is the most basic means by which to explain how God operates. God commands everything He wants to materialize in the heavens and on earth and uses Jesus, His Holy Spirit, His Heavenly angels and man to insure His will is accomplished. He is a God of order. He never circumvents His ranks.

God is the originator of all creativity, powers, and change. He is the supreme, infinite and power source of the universe.

Truth: There is nothing too big or impossible for God! Jesus stated: *"With men it is impossible, but not with God: for with God all things are possible"* (**Mark10:27**).

Simply put, God gives the instructions, and Jesus tells the Holy Spirit the concepts used in Chapters 2: who, what, where, when, why, and how. Love is why Jesus promised to send the Holy Spirit to the disciples in the 14th chapter of John. He also expressed to the disciples why obedience to His commands is crucial and a must. Jesus said:

"If you love me, obey my commandments and I will ask the Father and he will send you another Advocate, who will never leave you. He is the Holy Spirit, who leads into all truths. The world cannot receive him, because it isn't looking for himanddoesn't recognize him. But you know him, because he lives with you now and later will be in you.

Soon the world will no longer see me, but you will see me. Since I live, you also will live. When I am raised to life again, you will you will know that I am in my Father, and you are in me, and I am in you. Those who accept my commandments and obey them are the ones who love me. And because they love me, my Father will love them. And I will love them and reveal myself to each of them" **(John 14:15-21)**.

The ministry of the Holy Spirit is divinely universal. His presence is all knowingly. The spiritual attributes of His power and presence is unsurpassed and is required for ministry. I believe you should not start a ministry without His anointing. Although, many launch their ministries without "waiting" for Jesus to send Him to empower those He has chosen... The Bible gives clear illustration and commanded the need to "wait" for Him (Acts:1-4).

The Role of the Holy Spirit Based on Jesus' Promise

Jesus said, "The Helper." The Father will send Him in My name.

1. He will abide with you forever.

2. He will be in you.

3. He will guide you into all truth.

4. He will glorify Christ.

5. He will help you.

6. He will comfort you.

7. He will teach you.

8. He will take of Christ and disclose to you what is to come (future).

9. He will not speak of His own, but only what He hears; He speaks from Christ.

10. He will bring to your remembrance all that Christ has said to you.

11. He will give you peace.

12. He will convict the world concerning sin.

Luke 4:18-19, (NKJV) tells us that when the Holy Spirit is upon you, according to Jesus you are:

1. Anointed (empowered) to preach the good news (gospel) to the poor (spiritually).

2. Anointed (empowered) to heal the brokenhearted (oppressed).

3. Anointed (empowered) to deliver those who are bruised (heal all sicknesses).

4. Anointed (empowered) to restore sight to the blind (physically and spiritually).

5. Anointed (empowered) to set the captives free (deliver from bondage).

6. Anointed (empowered) to preach the acceptable year of the Lord (every year).

These powers are the fundamental attributes that make up the Holy Spirit's character. His omnipotence, omnipresence, and omniscient abilities cover all of our needs for us to live a fulfilled Christian life while serving God and His people. I believe major consequences are exacted upon men and women who prematurely start ministries without receiving the power it takes to carry them through the spiritual battles. They will not have the ability to withstand the demonic forces that oppose Christ; **will** come against their family, ministry, and faith.

In Luke, Jesus explained to the apostles about receiving the Holy Spirit: *"But you will receive the powers when the Holy Spirit has come upon you; and you shall be My witnesses both in Jerusalem, and in all Judea and Samaria, and even to the remotest part of the earth"* **(Acts 1:8).**

Jesus knew how important the Holy Spirit is for the journey of ministry. I will reiterate again, He said, "Wait for the Holy Spirit (Power) so you can be My witnesses." He has to approve you and me as His witnesses and will empower us with His Holy Spirit before we go in the world to minister. There's also the adverse consequence of receiving the Holy Spirit and waiting too long to start our ministries. Souls are lost to the Lord and people are remaining in bondage when we do not obey. According to the Book of Acts, Jesus told the apostles not to leave Jerusalem, but to wait for Him to send the gift of the Holy Spirit.

Gathering them together, He commanded them not leave Jerusalem, but to wait for what the Father had promised, "Which," He said, "you heard of Me; for John baptized with water, but you will be baptized with the Holy Spirit not many days from now" **(Acts 1:4).**

Many believers have been baptized in the Holy Spirit and have not budged from their perches. They have been empowered to: preach the Gospel, heal the sick, deliver the bruised, free those in bondage, and restore sight, but they are scared or living in doubt, which is sin. This Scripture is not a suggestion, it is a command of Jesus. He said:

"Go ye there for and make disciple of all the nations, baptizing them in the name of the Father and the Son and the Holy Spirit, teaching them to observe all that I commanded you; and lo, I am with you always, even to the end of the age" **(Matthew 28:19-20).**

Chapter Ten
Faith to Love and to Be Loved

Love is the most powerful force on earth. This paradoxical- dichotomy of divine or destructive emotion can literally create or destroy anything in its path. I have deduced with absolute truth the answers to some of our greatest challenges in this **most** important chapter. I pray that you earnestly examine the core of where you really are in your relationships in this moment of reality. Before I move any further into this exciting discourse of information, I want to compel you to search spiritually, momentarily (just 5 minutes) to prepare for a journey of truth about true love and how you might find that one and only true-non-evasive lover we all have been searching for is Christ!

Once you find His kind of love, every door to creativity and opportunity will swing open and you will become a magnet for love and success in every arena you desire to endeavor, it is a guarantee! Amazing enough but not surprisingly, we are not taught in our early years the order of love. Godly love has basic fundamental behavior standards that must be applied and in no way compromised. True love is governed by **Two Laws** of nature that will never be mutually beneficial

If they are practiced or eradicated continuously with determination and caution, you will never fail love and love will never fail you. These laws are the regulators of human nature and they direct your course for a rich or poor life.

All roads to success or failure hang on these two '*spiritual laws*.' Now that I have your attention I will proceed...

Have you ever gotten ahead of love to realize I have taken the wrong road to lust? In 1984, the rock and roll singer Tina Turner staged one the 'greatest comebacks' in recording history. The song was called "What's Love Got to With It." Little did she know that this record would catapult her to stardom beyond all of her previous years in the music business! Why is the word "love" so powerful? What innately drives man to fulfill his greatest desire with the attraction of such force he is often guided or misguided with the imagination of euphoric fantasy?

It has been documented in the pages of history of the stories of men and women accomplishing enormous feats because of the power of love. Likewise, we've heard of the men and women who have conquered great enemies and amassed immense wealth and some have also destroyed countless lives because of love. Love is the strongest craving of man to reach his maximum potential. This is true in religion as well as universally—the word love has the same power.

The apostle John wrote one of the most powerful verses in the Bible. This scripture of course is from a spiritual, personal and relational experience of God's love for man through Jesus. He had firsthand knowledge of,"What's Love Got to Do With It" from God. He wrote:

"For God so loved the world that He gave his "Only Begotten Son," that whosoever believes in Him shall not perish but have everlasting life" (John 3:16).

What is love? This is such a broad question! According to Webster's dictionary, love is: (1) A deep tender, ineffable feeling of affection and solicitude toward a person, such as arising from kinship and recognition of attractiveness, fondness, tenderness, warmth, intimacy, attachment and endearment. (2) A desire to want to be in the presence of the ones we love.

There are many similar man-conjured meanings of love but they are only minuscule descriptions at best of what we think or feel about this powerful word. Honestly, there were not any definitions that I could appropriately and adequately give meaning to the broadness and endless thoughts of what this word truly means. Just as God has no expressible words because of His deity and supremacy, love is comparable to God, it cannot be explained. John stated, "God so love the world" that He gave...When we say I love you and there is no godly exchange, we do not love.

Now, if God gave us faith and He did! *He expects us to target our faith in love and our love in faith.*

These two combined together are practically the divine supernatural creative principles in the universe and they are limitless in their power. Love and faith are central components to the supreme power of God. There are many Scriptures written in the Bible regarding "love" but the one that destroys every scheme, devices and atmospheric demonic power is all contained in the first Epistle of John. He wrote: *"There is no fear in love; but perfect love cast out all fear, because fear involves punishment; and the one who fears is not perfect in love"* (1 John 4:18).

God loves us so much that He sent 'Jesus' in the flesh to display and demonstrate His love and power and glory on earth. The apostle John experienced this personally for three and a half years; walking and talking with Jesus (Love) daily. There is no greater testimony we need other than to believe in Him. If we can grasp the true power of God's love without trying to be religious and target our passions of godly love with faith, nothing can be denied us. Love is universal and every human being desires to experience it. The demonic forces have absolutely no control over this power.

Love is so powerful that one man by the name of Mahatma Gandhi (former political Indian leader) was able to use principles of love without firing a single shot of ammunition to liberate an Indian Nation of 200 million people from British rule.

He was quoted saying:

"Love never claims, it ever gives; love never suffers, never resents, never revenges itself. Where there is love there is life; hatred leads to destruction." - **Mahatma Gandhi**

His words strongly remind us of the 13th Chapter of 1st Corinthians familiarly referred to as "The Love Chapter." Although Gandhi never embraced the Christian faith, he obviously studied and mastered the basic tenets of this thing called love. Jesus is love, personified and perfect in all of His grandeur. John gives a great and wonderful pointed statement. He wrote:

"Beloved, let us love one another, for love is God; and everyone who loves is born of God and knows God. The ones who do not love do not know God" **(1 John 4:7-8).**

Jesus set the ultimate example of how to truly love. It requires faith in the most basic and common way. However, the moment we subject ourselves to "love and to be loved," faith will target our heart towards the ones we love and their desires. Faith will always include love as well as others. Jesus could easily cast demons out wherever he went because He was perfect in His love.

For this reason, "cast" is depicted with Jesus healing those who were oppressed by the devil. He is the embodiment of love, faith and power. No demon can stand against the power of love, because the presence of love and hate (lust) cannot occupy the same space. Therefore the demons and hate have to leave. Remember Judas when he betrayed Jesus? When the devil entered his body he immediately left the room. He couldn't face the power of love within the Son of God.

In recounting the incident John wrote:

"Jesus responded, it is the one to whom I give the bread I dip in the bowl." And when he had dipped it, he gave it to Judas, son of Simon Iscariot. When Judas had eaten the bread, Satan entered into him. Then Jesus told him, "Hurry and do what you're going to do." None of the others at the table knew what Jesus meant. Since Judas was their treasurer, some thought Jesus was telling him to go and pay for the food or to give some money to the poor. So Judas left at once, going out into the night (John 13:26-27).

Faith to love means: I will open my heart with wisdom and understanding and expose myself to love and to be loved based on biblical principles and standards demonstrated by Christ. Society has placed such diminutive value on the true meaning of love. It is not a feeling for a season, or a reason or some exhilarated cosmos of ecstasy.

Love can become all God intended it to be through the examples and actions exhibited by Christ and those expressed so eloquently by the apostle Paul in the 13 chapter of 1st Corinthians. He wrote:

"Love is patient, love is kind and is not jealous; love does not brag and is not arrogant, does not act unbecoming; it does not seek its own, is not easily provoked, does not take into account a wrong suffered., does not rejoice in unrighteousness, but rejoices in the truth; bears all things, believes all things, hopes all things, endures all things. Love never fails; but if there are gifts of prophecy, they will be done away; if there are tongues, they will cease; if there is knowledge, it will be done away. For we know in part and we prophecy in part; but when the perfect comes, the partial will be done away. When I was a child, I used to speak like a child, think like a child, reason like a child; when I became a man, I did away with childish things. For now we see in a mirror dimly, but then face to face; now I know in part, but then I will fully just as I also have been fully known. But now faith, hope, love, abide these three; but the greatest of these is love" (1 Corinthians 13:4-13).

Paul's summation of love epitomizes and encapsulates the essence of God's kind of love. The very evidence of His agape love is established in the Bible from Genesis to Revelation. As we mature in the principles and standards set forth in His word, we will begin to be mirror images of His love reflecting the very nature and character of who He is. Because of God's love for us Christ died for our sins and purchased the contract of eternal death. We, too, must become living and viable manifestations of God's kind of love in this perishing and spiritually dying world.

It is our obligation as Christians to represent love, mercy and grace working in us through Jesus Christ. Most people never really experience true love. We have such warped demonstrations and expressions of what God's kind of love involves. The quest to discover true love is so prevalent that society has moved away from a clear sense of what godly love is. The masses have adopted views of distorted, ego-driven passions dressed and disguised as love, but bares all of the evidence of insensitive and erotic disdain of self-adulation and personal satisfaction.

The fashion of it all has the labeling and characteristic of loves counter-partner called, lust! Unlike love, lust never exhibits evidence of the real thing or godly love wrapped in faith. Many times we confuse love with various levels of lust which has insatiable destructive attributes that cannot be quenched or satisfied regardless of its momentary or superficial pleasures. The world says: "I love you, but I am not *in-love* with you!" What does this mean? What if God said, "For I, so *in-loved* the world that I gave My only begotten Son"... The definition of *in* is: A state of condition that something or somebody is experiencing.

In other words *in* means: cutting-edge, fashionable, trendy, hip, happening, vogue, now and short-lived. This type of so-called love is temporary and subject to change based upon feelings and circumstances.

For example, Director, Robert Townsend, filmed a scene in the movie, "The Five Heart Beats" between his character (Duck) and his brother (J.T.). Ducks soon-to-be wife was trying to explain to J.T. the feelings (lust) she had for the both of them. She was having a sexual affair with both brothers.' J. T. insisted she could not marry Duck, he felt she loved him because they too, were having an affair. He said, "I can't let you marry my brother because you love me, I know it because I've been with you." She said: "I love you J. T., but I am in-love with Duck!" *Was she "In-Lust?" Or did she in-love them both?*

This statement and behavior presents a major dilemma and is the same attitude that permeates the mentality of our culture today. Does God love us or does He *in-love* with us? No, <u>she was in lust!</u>

If God is *in-love* with us?Then, He can be *out-of-love* with us? In-love says: If you make me happy today and I feel good; I will love you! Or, if I am not happy today I will not! True love is not a fleeting feeling nor does its action contradict God's standards, principles and love. Lust is why so many marriages and relationships end in disarray or divorce. In the Grecian culture there are four words they defined as love: Eros, Phileo, Agape and Stogay. The Grecian's were once considered one of the most advanced nations on earth. Many of world's political, judicial, cultural and humanitarian systems originated from their concepts and philosophies. However, their sophistication was no match for the inherent godly desire man pursues in search for God's kind of love.

Eros, is sexual (lustful) or romantic love...essentially, the sexual behavior act is the correct expression of Eros; it is the love of the admirable, and it is a love that desires to control and influence negatively. Eros is measured as attractive and desirable by the subject, in so much with the accompanying feelings of compulsion to have power over its victim eventually causing major duress.

Phileo, a word used to illustrate companionship and sincere friendship that's developed and cultivated between two or more people who have genuine brotherly love and care for another. This form of love carries an unbreakable bond that is strengthened as time and challenges are experienced. It is often and can resemble but should not be mistaken for *Agape love.*

Agape, is the deepest form of love, which is based on God's principles, standards, and actions towards one another. Agape is a giving love, a love of freedom and a love of liberty. It connotes provisions and visions.

It presents hope and promotes life. It denounces self-gratification to announce others satisfaction. The early Christian believers continued demonstrating agape love by giving to those less fortunate.

God set the greatest example in giving us His Son on the cross. As a result, when we view the cross we should see God's effort to give unselfishly the most precious gift He could by sending His Son for us to have eternal life. It is this divine display of selflessness that we learn true godly love exhibited by the actions to always give sacrificially of ourselves.

The last and rarely used word is **Stogay,** which is the love of family and kindred. This love is so encouraging since, it's the type that connects families together so that, regardless of what external powers come against them, the cohesiveness of the group will remain intact to insure an indestructible bond. Although the family may suffer heartache and pain they will overcome the experience because of their unity. It's not a commonly used word and only appeared in the Scripture as a compound word. However, Greek mythologists and philosophers were exploring every method of expressing their culture's intimate feelings to discover love which is still to most a mystery—to all who venture into the timeless and unknown stratospheres of the word we call love.

Paul makes the distinction elementary in 1st Corinthians 13... nonetheless, our sexed-crazed society is in total denial and deception due to the pervasive and prevalent over-exposure and exploitation of sex by the media. We have allowed this attitude and behavior to dictate and devalue the meaning and purpose of genuine Agape/Godly love and have adopted Eros/lust as a social standard.

The danger of this vacillating, wavering and unstable behavior carries no permanent commitment, but straddles the fence of using the term "in-love" as a tool for control, manipulation and ungodly persuasions. This is what I refer to as, revolving and conditional love. It is totally contrary to the unconditional love Jesus taught and demonstrated. Lust can never be trusted and will take a turn and run at the moment of indifference or disagreement.

In the Book of Amos this Scripture is often used out of context not purposely, I believe, but carelessly. Most people misquote, "Agree" He wrote: "How can two walk together accept they agreed" **(Amos 3:3)**. This type of in-love has not *agreed* with the concerns of others. It is only concerned with what is good for "me, myself and I." Agreed means: decided settled, arranged, approved, fixed, granted, established and contracted or covenant. In essence, the word "agreed" should be used in a past-tensed context! This modern day *in-love* attitude demonstrates and has produced the highest divorce rate in recent history.

It breeds and has now birth the mentality, behavior, and new a phrase called: '*I am doing me!*' The phrase "I am doing me" is simply stating: It is all about *I, me,* and *my* desires and wants. They are selfish, egoistical and lustful in nature and spirit. The apostle Paul *tries* to explain this exhibition of two **(Laws)** natures warring against one another, he expounds: *"For we know that the Law is spiritual, but I am flesh, sold into bondage to sin. For what I am doing, I do not understand; for I am not practicing what I would like to do, but I am doing the very thing I hate. But if I do the very thing I do not want to do, I agree with the Law confessing that the Law is good.*

So, now no longer am I the one doing it, but sin that dwells in me. For I know that nothing good dwells in me, that is, in my flesh; for the willing is present in me, but the doing of the good is not. For the good that I want, I do not do, but I practice the very evil that I do not want. But if I am doing the very thing I do not want, I am no longer the one doing it, but sin which dwells in me. I find then the principle that evil is present in me, the one who wants to do good" (**Romans 7:14-21**).

When I, Fray White, am doing me, lust has overtaken my spirit and I am driven by my passions to be in complete control. There is nothing that will satisfy those desires of my lust, but sin. The letter "I" in the word 'sin' is always synonymous with the flesh. Paul did his absolute best trying to explain how he too wrestled with these two **laws**. We will also experience the same confusion as Paul did until we are able to control and eliminate the selfish conditions that accompany the lustful attributes of the flesh.

The word **lust** means: A strong physical desire to have sex usually without associated feelings of love, and affection or having uncontrolled or illicit sexual desire or appetite; an intense or unrestrained sexual craving. An overwhelming desire or craving: a lust for power. Intense eagerness or enthusiasm: a lust for desires for life. We don't know precisely what Paul's challenges were but he was subject to fleshly temptations just as we are.

When **love** is described as a verb it denotes transitive **and intransitive characteristics of godly intentions and** accomplishments. These are both action words that refer to the continuation of a positive outcome towards the ones we love. In fact, love will always take into account the desires of their godly needs. Unfortunately, when **lust** is satisfied or goes unsatisfied, it stops and turns into hate.

I will state this again for those of you who will not accept this as truth!! **Unfortunately,** when lust is satisfied or goes unsatisfied it stops and turns into hate," always! Regardless of the outcome the recipient of lust will ultimately lose...

The lust driven person does not accept being denied or rejected unless they initiate the action or terminate the relationship on their basis and benefit. I will use the story of Joseph in the Bible as a classic example of lust; when it is either satisfied or unsatisfied. In the Book of Genesis we will see a perfect example of lust in action and the outcome. This same response is typical today as it was thousands of years ago. So, do not think you will get a different result, you will not! Lust is a spirit. It defies time, whether it is historical, modern or future. The results are imminent!

I highly suggest you consider an in-depth assessment of the truth and consequence of living in a lust filled relationship. The end result of lust must be taken seriously or you will be destined down a similar path of destruction, oppression or enslavement. Hopefully, it is the godly-love path that you choose and not succumb to the demise and vicious end of lusts ungodly demands. In the Book of Genesis this timeless story illustrates one classic consequence of the behavior of lust.

Moses wrote:

Joseph was a strikingly handsome man. As time went on, his master's wife became infatuated with Joseph and one day said, "Sleep with me." He wouldn't do it. He said to his master's wife, "Look, with me here, my master doesn't give a second thought to anything that goes on here —he's put me in charge of everything he owns. He treats me as an equal.

The only thing he hasn't turned over to me is you. You're his wife, after all! How could I violate his trust and s i n against God?" She pestered him day after day after day, but he stood his ground. He refused to go to bed with her. On one of these days he came to the house to do his work and none of the household servants happened to be there. She grabbed him by his cloak, saying, "Sleep with me!" He left his coat in her hand and ran out of the house. When she realized that he had left his coat in her hand and run outside, she called to her house servants: "Look—this Hebrew shows up and before you know it he's trying to seduce us. He tried to make love to me but I yelled as loud as I could. With all my yelling and screaming, he left his coat beside me here and ran outside." She kept his coat right there until his master came home. She told him the same story. She said, "The Hebrew slave, the one you brought to us, came after me and tried to use me for his plaything. When I yelled and screamed, he left his coat with me and ran outside. "When his master heard his wife's story, telling him, "These are the things your slave did to me," he was furious. Joseph's master took him and threw him into the jail where the king's prisoners were locked up. But there in God was still with Joseph: He reached out in kindness to him; he put him on good terms with the head jailer (Genesis 39:6-23).

The Master's wife's behavior was just a symbolic act of coercion and endless ungodly demands. Her lust whether satisfied or unsatisfied resulted in the loss of liberty for Joseph and will cause comparable conditions if you encounter this spirit. Fortunately, God was with Joseph and turned it around, but it still caused him heartache. The number one indication is the consistent pestering of "Day after, day, after day" persistent ungodly demands. You must **define** the sixteen associated behaviors of lust listed later in this chapter (wrath, hate, adultery and etc.) to evaluate the devastating affects they will cause in your life.

Remember: "Day, after day, after day, after day, Run!!

Lust has no loyalty: once one of its insatiable behaviors has run its course it will quickly beckon another of its partners to enhance the chaotic actions. Lust will keep adding continually to each of its spirits to control the person or destroy them. Comparable to a mad scientist that keeps mixing one powerful toxic chemical with another until *he* or *she* has a deadly concoction of death. A lustful person will attempt to summon all sixteen of these negative behaviors until they eventually destroy its victim. You must acknowledge these pervasive actions and not allow yourself to compromise or even occupy the same space with a person you will suffer loses.

Joseph could have avoided this situation, remember: *Day, after day, after day!* Wow! If you are saying this to yourself or if you are in a similar situation, RUN!!! Because this sounds familiar does it not? I once dated a woman who pestered me *Day, after day, after day* , about having sex with her. When she could not have her way she would berate me, call me insulting names, would imply and question my sexuality. Nonetheless, this method of abuse is consistent with males or females.

These are indicators that you are not in a godly relationship. You must eradicate, terminate and move on. The Bible gives a true and simple checklist of how to distinguish between love and lust. The apostle Paul gives an exposition of why you cannot straddle the fence with these two ways of life in the Book of Galatians.

He wrote:

"My counsel is this: Live freely, animated and motivated by God's Spirit. Then you won't feed the compulsions of selfishness. For there is a root of sinful self-interest in us that is at odds with a free

spirit, just as the free spirit is incompatible with selfishness. These two ways of life are antithetical, so that you cannot live at times one way and at times another way according to how you feel on any given day. Why don't you choose to be led by the Spirit and so escape the erratic compulsions of a law-dominated existence? It is obvious what kind of life develops out of trying to get your own way all the time: repetitive, loveless, cheap sex; a stinking accumulation of mental and emotional garbage; frenzied and joyless grabs for happiness; trinket gods; magic- show religion; paranoid loneliness; cutthroat competition; all- consuming-yet-never-satisfied wants; a brutal temper; an impotence to love or be loved; divided homes and divided lives; small-minded and lopsided pursuits; the vicious habit of depersonalizing everyone into a rival; uncontrolled and uncontrollable addictions; ugly parodies of community. I could go on" **(Galatians: 5:16-21, NCB).**

If these examples are not enough the checklists below will help you to identify where you are in your relationships and friendships.

Love

Take a brief moment and use this check list as a gauge to view where you are presently in your life. Grab a writing utensil and truly mark off the attributes that you need to improve on and the ones that you are experiencing from those that love you. You must make a conscience effort to communicate with those you love and that love you to incorporate all nine of these attributes to have a fulfilling life and relationship with these type of people.

Please check-off for evaluation:

The Positive Attributes (Spirit of God)

1. Love_____
2. Joy _____
3. Peace_____
4. Patience (Long-Suffering) _____
5. Gentleness_____
6. Goodness_____
7. Faith_____
8. Meekness_____
9. Temperance_____

Note: The ultimate goal is to be able to check all the positive attributes.

The attributes of love are profound and in many ways simple to evaluate. Oftentimes, we live in self-denial and will not explore a conservative approach to consider whether we are experiencing this godly love that exposes us to a marvelous world of magnetic forces drawing unlimited creative powers, opportunities and pleasures from every godly source imaginable.

Love attributes can never be defied nor will they be denied. Love will always view the world as unlimited and all possible and will place no restraints on your ability to create because love does not *confine*, it *refines!*

Lust

Please view the list below and take a few moments to be honest and intentional regarding your friendships, relationships and more importantly yourself. You must place extreme and immediate emphasis to eradicate any of these sixteen lust behaviors from your life. You cannot compromise with anyone if they are a part of their lives. You will not experience long term success without the attributes and spirit of love, it is impossible.

Please check-off for evaluation:

The Negative Behaviors of Lust (Sin, Flesh, Me, Myself and I)

1. Adultery_____
2. Fornication_____
3. Uncleanness_____
4. Lasciviousness_____
5. Idolatry_____
6. Witchcraft_____
7. Hatred_____
8. Variance_____
9. Emulations_____
10. Wrath_____
11. Strife_____
12. Seditions_____
13. Heresies_____
14. Envying_____
15. Murders_____
16. Drunkenness_____

Note: The ultimate goal is to check off the negative behaviors and eradicate them all.

The behaviors of lust are real and **will** destroy you. Lust is a serious and dangerous spirit. Most of us will first look beyond ourselves and think about those we know who possess these behaviors. However, I am asking you to examine yourself and then those that you love. This self-evaluation, removes the plank out of your eyes before removing the speck from your loved ones or lust ones. In essence, do not judge them, but judge yourself!

All of the sixteen lust behaviors are rooted in demonic chaos and confusion and therefore compromise the possibility to be secure and foundational in the process of love and creativity. Conversely, the majority of man's fall can be traced directly to one or more of these **lust-filled** behaviors as the motivating factor to his or her failures. Unless you deal with these behaviors in your relationships or improve on the love attributes you are headed for disaster, failure and a life of mediocrity.

You cannot be consistently creative and focused if any of these behaviors of lust are prevalent. They are complementary to one another feeding and growing intrinsically dependent upon one another. Comparable to a forest and flame, fungus, algae or cancer they will eventually spread either like a wild fire or with a gradual and slow destructive purpose of destroying every living-creative-thought, vision or dream. These spirits are also cyclical and will cause the recipient to stay in a constant state of counter-productivity.

All of these lust behaviors are mind altering and have psychological and physiological combative traits that can render you hopeless. By purposely eliminating these lustful behaviors from every area of your life you will begin to see with clarity the success, freedom and true love God has abundantly planned for your life.

Godliness Draws True Love

The quest for true love will always be attainable for some, hopeless for others, and for many ever-elusive until we institute the correct process in which God has instructed for us through His word. The world as we live in it now, possesses some interesting challenges for those seeking true love. We have a litany of despairing circumstances that are statistically challenging for those who are looking for godly love. We have a changing mentality of what true love is and a mounting imbalance of available men for marital-mates to women who are waiting for men who desire to be married.

We have reached an epidemic state of frustration for many women whom are expressing their honest feelings regarding the availability of qualified suitors. The current economical, spiritual and immoral state of our society has drastically reduced the possibilities and opportunities for many of our women to experience matrimony. Moreover, I believe by the virtue of God that every woman who desires to be married will draw that future godly husband to her as a magnet compels steel, like bees to an orchard of rare sunflowers in early spring waiting for pollination—creating a natural sweetness in her as pure as golden honey.

For she's arrayed with such elegance and glory; as that one rare golden apple displayed amongst the red apples in a perfectly-painted-Picasso-portrait; glowing with such radiant beauty she cannot be opposed. No man can resist the magnetism of a godly woman. For she possesses a distinct calm spirit that exudes all of the attributes of love—as she instinctively, gracefully, and peacefully carries herself in such a manner as pleasing to God.

The Bible says, "He who finds himself a wife finds himself a good thing and has favor from the Lord" Proverbs (18:22). Can you image having favor from the Lord?

Favor from God is: His goodness, His support, His kindness, His grace, and His mercy.

The author of the Book "Fountain of Pleasures" wrote of the affect a man can have on a woman saying:

*"The sweetest women can be turned into a shrew by a man if he excites her but does not fulfill her. To tame her and to bring her back to sweetness he must make love to her and bring forth her pleasures, and she will turn immediately as night changes to day . . . She will then become a good wife, a good companion, a good mother, and a good human being."*Haroun Al Makhzoumi

The author said, "He must *make* love to her to bring out her pleasures." I will add my opinion saying, 'it must be based on godly love.' To **make** is to: create, craft, build, construct, compose and formulate. To **love** her godly, he must wash her in the Word of God continuously to bring forth her godly **pleasures** which are: love, joy, peace, meekness, gentleness, patience, faith, goodness and temperance which are all in the Spirit of Christ.

I charge the godly man to seek after his divine beauty of love with all of his heart in marriage and find her. And that he sees her as God does. I pray that he recognize she is his glorious gift from God that emanates the very essence of "What's Love Got to Do with It." Finally, because of his true love for her, he will gladly give himself to her as Christ gave Himself to the Church. If he truly does this, they both will believe and trust in one another to have the "Faith to Love and to Be Loved."

Chapter Eleven
Man was made to Create in Every Age

We must understand the phase "To Create." In the Book of Genesis, God began His infinite journey of creation by systematically calling out living substance and life from the deepest depths of a darkened, eerie and lifeless age of void. His divine methodical process of manifestation involved such planning and detail that our human logic cannot fathom the sheer awesomeness of His creation. It defies our human capacity to truly appreciate the magnificent grandeur of it all. God's earthly exhibits of marvels and wonders have withstood the test of climate changes, wars, plagues, and complete decimation of many cities and nations throughout the ages.

In every age man has neglected to do the will of God and have allowed His creative spirit inside of him to literally dissipate, rendering Him null and void in their lives; by denying the very purpose of God's creative power. Though many ages have passed and hopefully numerous others will, the basic fundamental purpose for man's presence on earth is to create (duplicate Christ). The power to create is usually a single thought from God and belief of an individual to capture the finite details of a dream, idea, vision or revelation with such clarity that he or she can actually see the end of creation before it ever reaches the planning stage.

Basically, the creator becomes enamored by faith and works that it's attainable without fail. Whether families, corporations or institutions—nothing can be built or created foundationally and fundamentally without the presence of "faith." In the Garden of Eden, God created a place for man to dwell and prosper. Adam and Eve were given full authority over everything in the Garden with one exception: not to eat of the **Tree of the Knowledge of Good and Evil**.

That very act of unfaithfulness set in motion an *age* of spiritual corruption, sin, and death. However, by the grace of God and Christ's redemption *age,* He restored our faith and empowered us to do even greater works; now, and in this present and in the ages to come. In other words, we are born to create by faith and by works!!

The Information (Big Data) Age

I believe we are in the greatest age in history! As a matter of fact, every age gets better if we view it as God does. Christians have the opportunity to spread *information* about Jesus around the world. The many methods we have through media, social media and networking has expanded our capability far beyond our imagination. Today, I am more excited about the future than ever before.

The definition for age is: era, period and times. We are in the most advanced age ever known to man. The only thing that will separate those that experience this phenomenon of success is *information*. In the information age you will create, service, sell or buy information (Data). Those who understand this fact will thrive. Those who ignore this fact may survive, but those who create WITH this fact in mind—will be alive.

I thank God that He has allowed me to live in such an age of possibilities. Information is so important that companies are starting to use the symbol *i* in their marketing campaigns which represents: **information.** This relatively new industry is destined to create a generation of possible trillionaires, who recently became billionaires, surpassing those that were millionaires, before they ever became thousanaires or hundrenaires.

I will repeat: We are in the information age... You will create information, service information, sell information or consume information. In essence, you will be a creator, participator or spectator...

The word **Data** is defined as: Information, statistics, facts, figures, numbers and records. Information is the growing demand of the future and we must all understand what roles we are going to play in able to capitalize ($$$) on its value. Data companies will be the power-brokers that control, manage and secure these commodities are going to continue to grow the net worth of their owners and investors as well as dictate the economic movement, monetary systems, political power, and global influence.

Unprecedented wealth is being produced with intangible and tangible assets of our personal and corporate data that we provided virtually for free or indirectly through subtle inquisition, and now being collected, transformed, processed and sold into usable *information* that creates opportunities for companies that understand the value of our data. We have classic examples of relatively new startup companies and their owner's earning billions of dollars in Breakneck Speed.

For example:

1. Mark Zuckerberg, co-founder of Facebook: 2004 Net Worth: 41.4 Billion (September 2015).

2. Reid Hoffman, co-founder of LinkedIn: 2003 Net Worth: 3.7 Billion (September 2015)

3. Jack Dorsey, co-founder of Twitter: 2006 Net Worth: 2.2 Billion (September 2015)

4. Steve Chen, co-founder(s) of YouTube, Founded: 2006 Net Worth: 350 Million

5. Chad Hurley, Net Worth: 400 Million

6. Jawed Karem, Founder of Instagram: 2010 Sold to Facebook 2012 for 1 Billion Net Worth 140 Million (September 2015)

7. Fray White, founder of Faither.com (2015) Net Worth: TBD

The wealth that these individuals have accumulated is because they are creators and participators and not spectators. They have derived their wealth from allowing us to enter our data to their sites in the form of a profile to analyze our activities, habits, behaviors and vital statistics we send and receive across their networks. More importantly, these free sites accumulate billions of users which has opened an entirely new form of marketing and business opportunities for a multiplicity of business endeavors. We have the same opportunities to create and participate in this phenomenon taking place in the *information* age. You must acknowledge that *information* is power.

We can no longer view these DATA companies as chat sites, but we must see the hidden mysteries of an industry that is creating corporations, jobs and wealth unseen before in recent history. My question to you is? When will you begin to create, participate or will you spectate in this age (*information*) of possibilities and unlimited opportunities.

Creator

The Internet is the new world (www) of commerce and wealth producing ventures. I listed previously people who have amassed great wealth in a relative brief period of time. You must not sit still and watch thousands of companies launch their virtual businesses with very little start-up capital or raise the funding they need with a clear and concise business model that investors are ready to throw large sums of money into.

The concept behind any virtual Internet business is to sell a product or service and generate Data Traffic (Visits) to and from your site. It is no different than a traditional brick and mortar store. By people visiting your site it generates a *Data Report* of how many times your site was viewed. This invaluable analysis (**analytics**) will allow you to use this information as a source of marketing opportunity for sales, customers, advertisers, products or services.

Email addresses and mobile phone numbers are the major vehicles into this new industry of business, opportunity and great wealth.

Important: You will never prosper in a **virtual world** trying to work in a **physical mindset**.

Examples of new startups to watch in 2015:

www.circa.com - Android App that tracks breaking news stories.

www.levelmoney.com - App that tracks your bank transactions.

www.routehappy.com- App to inform travelers of best seats, hotels and amenities

www.Flipboard.com - Apps that allow users to create own magazines for shopping.

www.Oyster.com - App to allow unlimited access to ebooks.

www.uber.com - International Ride sharing service

www.datasift.com - A Social Media analytics (DATA tracking) company.

www.clinkle.com - App that uses high frequency sound to process mobile payments.

www.circle.com - Apps that allow digital currencies like Bitcom.

www.smartthings.com - Tools that allow us to connect our smartphones with our homes.

These companies did not exist 5 years ago, but they are fast becoming major players in the information age.

When will you start your new company?

What is your idea?

How can I prosper? Glad you should ask. Participate!

Participator

How do I participate today? What skills do you possess at this moment and how can you market them on the Internet? What are you doing now at your job? Who are your friends? And what are their skills? I'm going to provide you with sites that will help you get established and ready for business. You have no excuse...

    A. Do you have a Website?

    B. Do you have a Domain name?

    C. Do you have an App?

    D. Do you have email address?

    E. Do you have a smartphone?

Domain Companies

www.godaddy.com

www.yahoo.com

www.domain.com

www.register.com

www.misk.com

Web Hosting Companies

www.godaddy.com

www.yahoo.com

www.wix.com

www.landl.com

www.fatcow.com

App Companies

www.theappcompany.com

www.play.google.com

www.nerdery.com

www.willowtreeapps.com

www.theymakeapps.com

Spectator

A spectator is one who looks and makes excuses for not creating and participating. If you desire to **_spectate_** in this wonderful world of opportunity, all you will need is a job, purse and wallet because it's your money and time that will finance the visions of these creators and participators. I have removed every excuse you may have to not create and participate. Therefore, by faith and your action start your journey into this **_age_** of information, opportunity and wealth to build a legacy for the kingdom of heaven, your family and the world.

In order to be a viable player you must have the tools that utilize these wealth producing sites and not use them for games, but as investment vehicles and learn to drive them to a successful location in our world of valuable data (*information*).

The iBook, iPad, iPod, iTunes, Nooks, Kindles, eBooks readers and other information sharing devices must become a primary part of your life in order to migrate into to these opportunities of wealth, convenience and relevance. The multiple excuses we have used in the past will no longer be an acceptable practice. These tools must be additions to your life.

Tools for the Age

Laptop, PC, iPad, Kindle, Nook, Tablets: A device or a computer is particularly marketed as a platform for audio-visual media, convenience and portability.

iPhone: Apple's first Internet-enabled Smartphone. It combines the features of a mobile phone, wireless Internet device, and iPod into one package.

iTunes: A proprietary digital media player application, used for playing and organizing digital music and video files.

eBooks: An amazing way to download and read books. E-books represent 30 % of all book sales in 2015. Also, they cost 50% percent or less than printed books to include many free book offers.

Smart Phones: i.e. Androids and other data devices such as: laptops, desk top computers and other computing devices.

GPS: Global Positioning System: A device or application (available on most smart phones) that gives invaluable audio or visual geographical data for terrain, mileage, travel time, preferred route and etc... pertaining to commercial, residential and business features.

Personal and Corporate Website or Webpage: A media site or page (s) that brands you personally or corporately. It's comparable to a Media Business Card.

Eventually popular sites are going to charge a service fee to host your information. I believe it's a matter of time. So, you might as well learn to develop your own as well as update them as your status changes. There are numerous web design companies that will allow you to develop a website or page (s) and will host it for a monthly fee. Your website or page (s) must describe your expertise, education, experiences and skill sets.

In other words: You must become synonymous with a thought, phase, word, craft or place when people refer or think of you.

Apps: A self-contained program or software designed to fulfill a particular purpose; used primary with mobile phones and web pages as a one touch function and icon (synonymous) button to identify a person, place or thing.

I believe we will all need our own personal apps eventually. They are convenient and serve as a one-stop-shop button for direct access to your personal or corporate page for accessing and retrieving your information, (data) products and services.

For example:

Billy Graham: Evangelist

Steve Jobs: Apple

Warren Buffet: Wealth

Bill Gates: Microsoft

Michael Jordon: Basketball

Oprah Winfrey: Media

Tiger Woods: Golf

Fray White: Faith

Now, what happens if you stay in the past and refuse to enter into our world where information and resources are being transmitted and distributed using data devices and media pages and you do not have one? It is comparable to a horse verses a car. You will always arrive too late to participate. I urge you now, to move into this marvelous world of technology and become an active creator deeply involving yourself in the revolution of information. Information is here to stay and those that understand information's worth will increase their net worth and influence. Meaning: to be fruitful, multiply and dominate.

The Gettysburg Address

It was Thursday November 19, 1863, in the middle of a war torn field where thousands of men died fighting for liberty and a better way of life for all people that he delivered the infamous Gettysburg Address, former President Abraham Lincoln stood tall and humbled himself on sacred grounds and stated:

Four score and seven years ago our fathers brought forth on this continent a new nation, conceived in liberty, and dedicated to the proposition that all men are created equal. Now we are engaged in a great civil war, testing whether that nation, or any nation, so conceived and so dedicated, can long endure. We are met on a great battle-field of that war. We have come to dedicate a portion of that field, as a final resting place for those who here gave their lives that that nation might live. It is altogether fitting and proper that we should do this.

But, in a larger sense, we cannot dedicate, we cannot consecrate, we cannot hallow this ground. The brave men, living and dead, who struggled here, have consecrated it, far above our poor power to add or detract. The world will little note, nor long remember what we say here, but it can never forget what they did here. It is for us the living, rather, to be dedicated here to the unfinished work which they who fought here have thus far so nobly advanced.

It is rather for us to be here dedicated to the great task remaining before us—that from these honored dead we take increased devotion to that cause for which they gave the last full measure of devotion— that we here highly resolve that these dead shall not have died in vain—that this nation, under God, shall have a new birth of freedom—and that government of the people, by the people, for the people, shall not perish from the earth.
(The Gettysburg Address-1863)

America and other nations have gone through many ages since that speech and today we have some of the same problems that still exist as they did during that age.

"Man Was Made to Create in Every Age!"

It will never be the responsibility of our government to solve our problems: We must!

The prophet Isaiah stated it rather plainly saying:

"For a child will be born to us, a son will be given to us: And the government shall rest on His shoulders; And His name will be called Wonderful, Counselor, Mighty God, Eternal Father, Prince of peace. There will be no end to the increase of His government or of peace" **(Isaiah 9:6-7).**

It is a Christian's responsibility to create a nation that shoulders the responsibility and provide the *needs of, for, and by the people.* We cannot sit idle and expect the government to care for the masses. It will not happen. A true servant of the people understands that it is his or hers obligation to God to be the difference and be the solution. Ninety-eight years after President Lincoln addressed Gettysburg we were still confronted with many of the same needs and they will never change unless we as Christians do our part.

President Kennedy's Inaugural Speech

On January 20, 1961, President John F. Kennedy in his inaugural speech to the nation spoke to an entirely different age of people, but with similar needs and concerns.

He said:

Vice President Johnson, Mr. Speaker, Mr. Chief Justice, President [1] *Eisenhower, Vice President Nixon, President Truman, reverend clergy, fellow citizens, we observe today not a victory of party, but a celebration of freedom—symbolizing an end, as well as a beginning—signifying renewal, as well as change. For I have sworn before you and Almighty God the same solemn oath our forebears prescribed nearly a century and three quarters ago.*

The world is very different now. For man holds in his mortal hands the power to abolish all forms of human poverty and all forms of human life. And yet the same revolutionary beliefs for which our forebears fought are still at issue around the globe—the belief that the rights of man come not from the generosity of the state, but from the hand of God.

We dare not forget today that we are the heirs of that first revolution. Let the word go forth from this time and place, to friend and foe alike, that the torch has been passed to a new generation of Americans— born in this century, tempered by war, disciplined by a hard and bitter peace, proud of our ancient heritage— and unwilling to witness or permit the slow undoing of those human rights to which this Nation has always been committed, and to which we are committed today at home and around the world.

Let every nation know, whether it wishes us well or ill, that we shall pay any price, bear any burden, meet any hardship, support any friend, oppose any foe, in order to assure the survival and the success of liberty.

This much we pledge—and more.

To those old allies whose cultural and spiritual origins we share, we pledge the loyalty of faithful friends. United, there is little we cannot do in a host of cooperative ventures. Divided, there is little we can do— for we dare not meet a powerful challenge at odds and split asunder.

To those new States whom we welcome to the ranks of the free, we pledge our word that one form of colonial control shall not have passed away merely to be replaced by a far more iron tyranny. We shall not always expect to find them supporting our view. But we shall always hope to find them strongly supporting their own freedom—and to remember that, in the past, those who foolishly sought power by riding the back of the tiger ended upinside.

To those peoples in the huts and villages across the globe 8 struggling to break the bonds of mass misery, we pledge our best efforts to help them help themselves, for whatever period is required—not because the Communists may be doing it, not because we seek their votes, but because it is right. If a free society cannot help the many who are poor, it cannot save the few who are rich.

To our sister republics south of our border, we offer a special 9 pledge—to convert our good words into good deeds—in a new alliance for progress—to assist free men and free governments in casting off the chains of poverty. But this peaceful revolution of hope cannot become the prey of hostile powers. Let all our neighbors know that we shall join with them to oppose aggression or subversion anywhere in the Americas. And let every other power know that this Hemisphere intends to remain the master of its own house.

To that world assembly of sovereign states, the United 10 Nations, our last best hope in an age where the instruments of war have far outpaced the instruments of peace, we renew our pledge of support—to prevent it from becoming merely a forum for invective—to strengthen its shield of the new and the weak—and to enlarge the area in which its writ may run.

Finally, to those nations who would make themselves our 11 adversary, we offer not a pledge but a request: thatboth sides begin anew the quest for peace, before thedark powers of destruction unleashed by science engulf all humanity in planned or accidental self-destruction.

We dare not tempt them with weakness. For only when
our arms are sufficient beyond doubt can we be certain
beyond doubt that they will never be employed.

But neither can two great and powerful groups of nations
take comfort from our present course—both sides
overburdened by the cost of modern weapons, both rightly
alarmed by the steady spread of the deadly atom, yet both
racing to alter that uncertain balance of terror that stays the
hand of mankind's final war.

So let us begin anew—remembering on both sides that
civility is not a sign of weakness, and sincerity is always
subject to proof. Let us never negotiate out of fear. But let
us never fear to negotiate.

Let both sides explore what problems unite us instead
of belaboring those problems which divide us.

Let both sides, for the first time, formulate serious and
precise proposals for the inspection and control of arms—and
bring the absolute power to destroy other nations under the
absolute control of all nations.

Let both sides seek to invoke the wonders of science
instead of its terrors. Together let us explore the stars,
conquer the deserts, eradicate disease, tap the ocean depths,
and encourage the arts and commerce.

Let both sides unite to heed in all corners of the earth the
command of Isaiah—to "undo the heavy burdens ... and to
let the oppressed go free."

And if a beachhead of cooperation may push back the
jungle of suspicion, let both sides join in creating a new
endeavor, not a new balance of power, but a new world of
law, where the strong are just and the weak secure and the
peace preserved.

All this will not be finished in the first 100 days. Nor will 20 it be finished in the first 1,000 days, nor in the life of this Administration, nor even perhaps in our lifetime on this planet. But let us begin.

In your hands, my fellow citizens, more than in mine, will 21 rest the final success or failure of our course. Since this country was founded, each generation of Americans has been summoned to give testimony to its national loyalty. The graves of young Americans who answered the call to service surround the globe.

Now the trumpet summons us again—not as a call to bear 22 arms, though arms we need; not as a call to battle, though embattled we are—but a call to bear the burden of a long twilight struggle, year in and year out, "rejoicing in hope, patient in tribulation"—a struggle against the common enemies of man: tyranny, poverty, disease, and war itself.

Can we forge against these enemies a grand and global 23 alliance, North and South, East and West, that can assure a more fruitful life for all mankind? Will you join in that historic effort?

In the long history of the world, only a few generations 24 have been granted the role of defending freedom in its hour of maximum danger. I do not shrink from this responsibility—I welcome it. I do not believe that any of us would exchange places with any other people or any other generation. The energy, the faith, the devotion which we bring to this endeavor will light our country and all who serve it—and the glow from that fire can truly light the world.

And so, my fellow Americans; ask not what your   25
country can do for you-ask what you can do for your
country.

Finally, whether you are citizens of America or   26
citizens of the world, ask of us the same high standards
of strength and sacrifice which we ask of you. With a
good conscience our only sure reward, with history the
final judge of our deeds, let us go forth to lead the land
we love, asking His blessing and His help, but knowing
that here on earth God's work must truly be our own
(The Presidential Inaugural Speech-1961).

Former President Kennedy said:

*"With a good conscience our only sure reward is, with history the
final judge of our deeds, let us go forth to lead the land we
love, asking His blessing and His help, but knowing that here on
earth God's work must truly be our own."*

I will repeat one of the greatest statements in the history of
a free and civilized nation. President Kennedy said;

*"And so, my fellow Americans: ask not what your country
can do for you—ask what you can do for your country. My
fellow citizens of the world: ask not what America will do for
you, but what together we can do for the freedom of man."*

It is my desire that you truly read these timeless speeches
stored in the archives of our country's history. They are still
just as relevant today as they were the day they
flowed effortlessly from the mouth of a tall, lanky, stoic and

unassuming man on a once blood soaked field at Gettysburg. I'm sure he could sense the presence of the souls of soldiers on both sides of political and moral differences who fought and died for what they believed, were still present on that afternoon. Years later in Washington, DC stood a young fearless new leader in freezing temperatures to address an embattled nation needing hope and security.

He did not disappoint, rather he gave us a mandate and a charge to serve. These two great men gave their lives for the freedom and liberty of a nation and world. They both knew the possible dire consequences of their actions in a time when violence, hate, hopelessness, threats of war, racism, political indifferences and poverty reigned supreme. Often with the threat of death looming constantly; knowing any day could be their last. They pressed on to serve a nation they loved. How far have we really advanced? What can you do to make the world a better place? And when are you going to do it?

In essence, you and I are the solution to the world's problems and we must accept it today. We are experiencing major financial and humanitarian issues in North America, South America, Europe, Asia, Africa, Afghanistan, Iraq, Libya, Syria, Mexico and all other nations. Without the presence of peace and prosperity our countries will never truly experience freedom to create nations conducive for long term success and harmony. We must establish governments of unity, love and peace for the citizens to begin living a life of faith. Fear and control kills the faith of any nation. God created man to be unlimited in his ability to create.

When countries are ruled by individuals (dictators) who deny the creative spirit of the people by suppressing their ability to create, it kills the nation. Our God is infinite in power! We are made in His image and therefore should never be restricted from exercising our freedom to create godly. For centuries the Chinese people were not allowed by their leaders to express their individual creativity until recently. In less than ten years they are fast becoming the dominate world power because they have unleashed their creative liberty and now allow their people to express their visions...

America was founded and built on biblical principles but we have become a cesspool of filth and ungodly creators. This is a major violation of God's laws and is causing chaos in our once God feared country. We are in a new age and we as creators must understand the needs of our citizens. It is a statistical fact that two percent of the American's control ninety percent of the wealth in the US. The emerging problem with this imbalance is the have not's confuse this as the have's monopolizing the resources when the only thing that separates the two is creativity, knowledge, action and sacrifice.

You must understand the *age* for what is significant in order to prosper and make a measurable difference for mankind. Oftentimes, we have no idea of the *age* and therefore fall deeper into the doldrums of irrelevance and become a by product of the past. Regardless of when we're born, the earth has been created and prepared for man's (your) arrival and inhabitance. We are to become proactive with faith and works to use the gifts we have in continuing the divine purpose of God's plan. Just as God "formed" Adam and Eve from the earth and gave him instructions and directions in caring and enhancing the earth for His glory. You and I were formed in the womb and introduced in the earth for a specific purpose in this age.

In the Book of Jeremiah he wrote of his vision and the statement God spoke to him, saying:

"I knew you before I formed you in the womb of your mother, before you came out I sanctified you and ordained you to be a Prophet to the nations" **(Jeremiah 1:5)**.

God is describing to Jeremiah the relationship they had prior to his arrival. Moreover, He is telling Jeremiah "I ordained and sanctified you to be a Prophet for this age." As we are birthed into this *age* it is not by happenstance, the word "knew" is a depiction of intimacy and prior relationship Jeremiah had with God. He was reminding the prophet of who he was before he lost his faith and purpose.

According to my dictionary the word *formed* is: The shape or structure of a thing that gives it its distinctive character, considered apart from its content, color, texture or composition. God's process of forming is as relevant now as it was in the past. He has a specific purpose for forming us in our mother's womb and introducing us into His earth. Again, God gave each of us "a measure of faith" (Romans 12:3).

Your faith will lie dormant until cultivated with the word of God and you agreeing with His original purpose for your life. God may have to reach forth and touch your mouth as He did to Jeremiah in verse nine, "Then the Lord reached forth and touched my mouth and said, "Look, I have put My words in your mouth" **(Jeremiah 1:9)**.

I believe Jeremiah was speaking doubt and God said, "Shut-up Jeremiah, your words are doubt and not faith" (Emphasis mine). Creativity is the apex of our existence and earthly purpose. Creativity marks a new beginning and where the word **"FAITH"** becomes relevant and palatable in our lives, **"NOW"**, and in the future. The word **"Faith"** has many definitions to the believer. As you focus on the evidence hoped for, **Faith** has already locked itself on the principle object of desire. The power of **Faith**, attraction and synergy is a universal law, once it is spoken and believed, it is comparable to the gravitational pull of the earth. No force on earth can negate this process of manifestation unless the believer doubts or either quits! In the Old Testament, there's a classic example of how two men and their **Faith** collided with belief and purpose and transcended *ages,* as they waited forty-five years for God's promise of **substance;** and the **evidence** to be fully manifested. In the Book of Numbers, the Lord spoke unto Moses saying:

"Send out for yourself men so that they may spy out the land of Canaan which I am going to give to the sons of Israel; you shall send a man from each of your fathers' tribes, everyone a leader among the" (**Numbers 13:1-4**).

Moses sent his defense minister Joshua, Caleb and ten other men to spy out the promise land. They spent 45 days roaming the hilltops and countryside observing the people (the sons of Anak were giants) in the land who were tall and mighty. Upon returning unto Moses and Aaron, the twelve men gathered around the people and said:

Thus they told him, we went into the land where you sent us, and it certainly does flow with milk and honey and this is the fruit" (*they brought back clusters of huge grapes for evidence*). *Nevertheless, the people who live there in the land are strong, and the cities are fortified and very large; moreover, we saw the descendants of Anak there. Then Caleb quieted the people before Moses and said; "we shall by all means go up and take possession of it, for we will surely overcome it"* (**Numbers 13:27-30**).

Caleb's faith never wavered as he commanded the doubter's to be quiet! He had walked the land of Canaan, and the vision of what God promised him never left his spirit. Whether he physically saw his desired promise or envisioned it, it was affixed in his mind and was still attainable.

The apostle John, during his revelation experience on the Island of Pathos wrote:

"And they overcame him by the blood of the Lamb (Christ) and the words of their testimony; and they loved not their lives unto death" **(Revelation 12:11).**

The commitment of faith for what one believes is often a life and/or death situation. In the case of Caleb and Joshua they were willing to risk their lives for what they were promised, believed and expected.

Their faith in possessing the Promise Land took precedence over their lives. Many men and women in all *ages* have sacrificed their lives believing in something they have never physically seen. Nonetheless, it was all too real in their minds. Their faith and the intangible manifestation was the motivating force burning within the depths of their beings.

True faith, is that tiny amber of trust in God, smoldering and waiting for that one slight fanning of air, in hope of igniting enough sparks to power the internal flame of their faith, to create a blaze that propels them to greater heights and greater glory. The story of Caleb is one of unending perseverance and faith. Upon entering the Promise Land he petitioned to Joshua with authority, for the land that God and Moses had promised him saying:

"Now, as you can see, the LORD has kept me alive and well as he promised for all this forty-five years since Moses made this promise— even while Israel wandered in the wilderness. Today I am eighty-five years old. I am as strong now as I was when Moses sent me on that

journey, and I can still travel and fight as well as I could then. So give me the hill country the Lord promised me. You will remember that as scouts we found the descendants of Anak living there in great, walled towns. But if the LORD is with me, I will drive them out of the land, just as the Lord said." So Joshua blessed Caleb son of Jephunneh and gave Hebron to him as his portion of land Hebron still belongs to the descendants of Caleb son of Jephunneh the Kenizzite because he wholeheartedly followed the Lord God of Israel **(Joshua 14:10-14)**.

Caleb's faith never waned or diminished. He remained vibrant, inspired and ageless, of possessing the land that was promised to him. **Faith** is a preserver and restorer. The Bible says, "he wholeheartedly" walked in all that God commanded. To understand "wholeheartedly," it simply means: the greatest extent possible or required. I will also list the synonyms as: enthusiastically, passionately, committed, unequivocally, unreservedly and totally. Caleb's flame of faith never extinguished and the hope of possessing the 'Promise Land' kept him youthful and strong.

You Must Have a Target in This Age

Caleb's testimony proves that age and faith has no limits. Believers should benefit from his testimony to remain valiant, expectant and courageous. By living a life of faith, we can live in excitement, expectation and maintain youthfulness, by focusing on what has been promised by God and fully believed. The stories of Caleb as well as others, who've exercised their faith, have one common denominator, a *Target!"*

Faithful people never lose focus of their desired substance!

After forty years in the wilderness and (which incidentally, was an 11 day journey) with all the distractions of life, war, death, idolatry, murmuring, and etc... He endured many things known to man, as we will, too! The master component of faith, that is common within the souls of all successful men and women, is they **Identify** and believe in a target. The word **"Target"** can also correlate with many other common words used today such as: **Goal, destiny, focus, vision, dream, aim, objective, mark,** and lastly, **End**.

The apostle Paul used the word "mark" in his Epistle to the Church at Philippi, he wrote:

"Brothers, I count not myself to have apprehended: but this one thing I do, forgetting those things which are behind, and reaching forth unto these things which are before. I press toward the mark for the prize of the high calling of God in Christ Jesus" **(Philippians 3:13-14)**.

Paul's faith was **targeted** on Christ! He did not concern himself with his past or present-day challenges because his focus was on that **"mark"** (which was Christ) and what God had revealed (vision) to him. Faith has to be directed at something specific, otherwise it is powerless. It is comparable to having the most powerful rocket on earth that can propel you into outer space, but it is stationed and pointed upward; never being launched to a specific (target) destiny.

Most people fail to experience faith on any major level. Why? They never have a "target." It is a simple principle that every human being must use. Faith has the potential of creating anything that you or I can imagine if we use the concepts and principles of its power. God has given to everyone aforementioned in the this book, "a measure of faith." It is not something reserved for the elite or the discreet.

Fact: Faith has no patents nor does it require any special-use permits!

It (Faith) only requires that you direct it to a "Target" and believe. What causes one person to harness the power of faith, while others seem to never truly grasp the basic concept of its reality? Faith gives us the ability to venture into the hidden dimensions of a new world yet seen, and bring back evidence of its existence. In the movie "The Passion of Christ," producer Mel Gibson gave the audience, 'those who had the experience of viewing it,' a great example of Jesus' life through film.

The film gave viewers a panoramic modern-day illustration of His brief journey on earth. We ventured theatrically down the stone roads to Bethlehem and witnessed the birth and introduction of the "The Baby Jesus," born to His virgin mother Mary. She knew from her *Conception* His obvious mission and target on earth was Calvary (The Cross). Gibson's movie was a marvelous effort in depicting and capturing the minds of the viewers to believe the re-enactment of His impending journey (Cavalry). Yet, Jesus knew His purpose and never allowed distractions or circumstances to alter his course of destiny.

In the Garden of Gethsemane, before heading to Calvary, (Jesus' Target) He became susceptible to earthly passions just as we do, in his moment of temptation. Written by Luke, He said to the disciples:

Pray that you may not enter into temptation. "And he withdrew from them about a stone's throw away, and knelt down and began to pray,

198

saying "*Father, if You are willing, remove this cup from Me; nevertheless, not My will, but Yours be done.*" *Now an angel from heaven came strengthening Him* **(Luke 22:40-42).**

In your moment of temptation (testing) you must stop and pray to God and focus on the vision and destiny He has promised you. He will send His angels, His Holy Spirit or a person with the truth (His word) you need to overcome that moment of weakness and refocus you on the "target." Just as Jesus considered for a moment, not finishing; His faith in God and the glory of heaven reminded Him of His "target" (Cavalry).

There will be many times you may want to quit and turn back, but faith, prayer and the "*target*"will keep your passion burning for the glorious finish.*Yes, again, there will be many times you will be discouraged and disappointed, but this example of how Jesus endured to the end should compel you towards the finish line.*

As Jesus prayed, the Bible says he was "*strengthened by the heavenly angel.*" Each time Jesus was tempted and needed regenerating He always resorted to prayer for strength and clarity. Prayer is a vitally important and essential part of keeping focused on the "target." Lastly, let's follow Jesus to His earthly target (Calvary) and experience His finish!

"Therefore when Jesus had received the sour wine, He said, "It is finished" and He bowed His head gave up His spirit"
(John 19:30, emphasis mine with underline).

There are countless biblical examples of faith and the outcome of people who trusted in God's promises. However, written, history for some believers is simply not enough. Unfortunately, in today's illusionary world, the media and film producers can create and duplicate wonders that leave their viewers in a state of belief, disbelief or doubt. These visual and audio techniques have created two interesting dilemmas: Productive (faith) and Counter-productive (doubt) causing entire generations to be divided and to wonder if miracles of faith still exist.

Our mind has the capacity to believe anything that is constantly presented to it, whether true or false or just entertainment. The film industry totally understands this phenomenon and the psychological impact it has on its viewers. Jesus also understood the importance of demonstrating anointed manifestations of heavenly powers to His disciples and followers. His ability to raise the dead, heal the sick, deliver the oppressed, work miracles, show signs, and do wonders validated Him as the Son of God. However, they continued to struggle with believing in (just as we do) His powers and wrestled with the authenticity of His earthly business.

As a child He visited the temple each Sabbath Day and was taught in the synagogues and learned from the Old Testament doctors, teachers and scholars of that (age) time. He also learned His carpentry skills from working in His earthly father's business (Joseph) the first 30 years of His life. He was perfecting His impending call to ministry. According to the Bible, on several accounts Jesus expressed His need to do business.

Jesus Doing Business in His Age

Luke describes how his mother and Joseph came back to Jerusalem in search for Jesus (he was boy) after he was not found with the caravan. They found Jesus in the temple being taught and asking questions. He wrote:

"And He said unto them, how is it that you look for me? Was I not about my Father's business?" **(Luke 2:49)**.

At the age of twelve, Jesus was serious and passionate about his business. Webster's definition of business is: purposeful activity; an immediate task or objective; action especially of an economic objective. In the Book of Proverbs Solomon expounds further concerning doing business. He wrote:

"Do you see a man skilled in his business, he will stand before kings he will not stand before obscure men" **(Proverbs 22:29)**.

Lastly, Solomon stated: *"For a dream comes through the multitude of business: and fool's voice is known by multitude of words"* **(Ecclesiastes 5:3)**.

Of course, Jesus and Solomon knew the importance of doing business. The wisdom and understanding that is obtained from the accumulation of diligence and prudence expands ones territory and opportunities. The impending question of today is how to make faith relevant in business today? As we read in the first chapter of Genesis, God has not changed his mandate of us to create.

You and I are the vehicles God uses to create changes in the ages. Although complex and broad as our world is today there are only three 'methods' of doing business. You will create, employ or be an employee in one or more of these methods and your level of understanding will determine your ability to adequately do business effectively with relative prosperity in this age.

These three methods are: **Products, Services and Information (Data)**. Contrary to biblical time's where agriculture once dominated the culture (age) and trade being second. As mankind evolves, change is inevitable and so does the needs of man. The agriculture, industrial, and technological age once revolutionized and shaped our world. Today we now have a new method (information).

Since the introduction of the computer, Internet and e-commerce, our businesses have changed forever. We have become a world of information senders, receivers and data bankers. This new age of information has streamed lined the concept of doing business within these three methods. However broad and diverse we have become, they still produce ten categories in which to do business. Below is a list of a few specialized categories within the three methods. Obviously, there are thousands others fields within these categories, but these listed below represent a microcosm of business opportunities within these three methods.

These categories' gives us a basic idea of how to determine where to *"Target"* our efforts now, with faith and works. Our present skills and knowledge base will identify our sphere of influence and ultimate success.

Ten Categories of Business

The ten categories of doing business, creating jobs and earning a living are:

1. Sales: (1) Highest paid (We all must become great sellers)

2. Exploration: Natural resources; oil, gold, silver, copper, etc...

3. Trade: barter, and partnerships for equal or greater value etc...

4. Service Providers: Ministry, Medical, law, accountants, plumbers etc...

5. Manufacturing: Cars, machinery, electronics, medical equipment etc...

6. Invention and R&D: Enhanced or improved existing products etc...

7. Intellectual Property: Information, books, film, music, entertainment etc...

8. Agricultural: Farming and Products from land and water i.e. fish etc.

9. Banking: Money, investments, interest, stocks, bonds and inheritance etc...

10. Lottery: Legalized gambling and state lotteries and odds at winning:

Match 5+ Powerball = 1:80,089,128
Match 5 = 1:1,953,393
Match 4+ Powerball = 1:364,042
Match 4 = 1:8,879
Match 3+ Powerball = 1:8,466
Match 3 = 1:207
Match 2+ Powerball = 1:605
Match 1+ Powerball = 1:118
Match Powerball = 1:74

You must do an honest assessment of where you are presently in your skill sets to determine your ability to gain employment or business opportunities within these categories. You must ask yourself: Can I prosper or am I qualified to prosper in these fields? Below is an evaluation checklist: I will use my skill sets as an example.

Check List:

1. Sales___X___
2. Exploration _____
3. Trade and Bartering___X___
4. Service___X_____
5. Manufacturing _____
6. Invention _____
7. Intellectual Property X_____
8. Farming, Agriculture and Fishing _____
9. Investments X____
10. Lottery_____I would not recommend this field.

The odds are always against you...

I currently have five ways to generate income, opportunity and growth in these arenas. Faith must be *targeted* towards the categories (fields) in which you have wisdom, knowledge and understanding. You must eliminate the categories that do not apply to your present skill sets (today) and concentrate on where you are 'now'! Remember, this is only a gauge for where you are presently and not where you are going.

Note: These fields of opportunity are always open for you once you determine to get educated, trained and experienced in specific areas of interest.

Truth: You must realize that you will rarely prosper in a field or profession that you refuse to master or acquire a degree, certification or expertise in. This is a major issue in the Christian community. We want to live prosperous lives but it cannot happen without attaining the understanding, knowledge and education we need to compete in these fields.

The rule of measure is comparable to getting a traditional Master's degree in a college. It requires discipline, time, and building your systems, networks and relationships (Chapter 6: God's Faith) of foundation and support. It does not happen overnight. It usually takes 5 to 7 years to truly get established in a new industry.

However, this process allows you to establish a good reputation of experience, reliability, respect, loyalty and trust with people in the industry that can help you become a success while learning and earning a good living.

Fact: You must pay your dues in any arena.

Solomon wrote: *"Trust in the Lord with all of your heart; do not depend on your own understanding"* **(Proverbs 3:5).**

This does not apply only to biblical knowledge. All knowledge emanates from God, He gives wisdom and understanding to men and women to share and teach others. Solomon is saying: once we "understand" our fields of endeavors through learning and experience we can become wise and over time can become experts.

Success is not being educated, but real success is having understanding of one's level education'. When deciding where to invest your expertise you must be detailed and specific with facts and demographic data, of meeting the needs of others.

Caution: *Faith works even when misguided to the wrong destiny!!*

There is no greater disappointment than to plan and invest your time, money and effort in the wrong arena. Careful planning and preparation must be strategic before launching into action (works). God and prayer will undoubtedly keep you focused on where God wants you to target your faith and works. The world is a much different place than what our parents and grandparents experienced.

Life is always moving forward and you must understand that God has equipped you and me to do some kind of business for Him while here on earth. He stated this fact rather plainly in the Book of Genesis when he said, 'Let us make man in our own image and our own likeness and He commanded us to fruitful, to multiply and to dominate" (Genesis 1:26). So, I encourage you to believe by faith and works that you have everything you need inside of you to begin creating the life God desires for you to live and continue to say to yourself, "I Was Made to Create in This Age!"

Chapter Twelve
Social Networking, Media and Technology

In today's modern language the buzzword for relationship building groups is "Social Networking and Media." Unfortunately, this current generation has diverted from traditional and personal communication and has adopted a non-intimate communicative way through social media and electronic technology such as texting, emailing and social- networking.

Wikipedia defines a social network as: *A social structure made up of individuals (or organizations) called "nodes", which are tied (connected) together by one or more specific types of group interdependency, such as friendship, kinship, common interest, financial exchange, dislike, sexual relationships, or personal relationships of beliefs, knowledge or prestige.*

Although, social networking, media and technology itself is not the culprit of miscommunication, certain aspects of electronic socializing create isolation, alienation and frustration for those not savvy enough to use these technologies or have access to them. The liability of this form of communication removes face-to-face dialog and the human factor.

Most importantly, it often compromises the effective inter-personal relations, truthfulness and clarity needed because of distorted and infrequent miscommunication.

Despite the fact that it's convenient, this type of messaging is causing major problems and indifferences with morals, integrity, and ethics unique only to social networking. Recently, we have experienced publically a wave of illicit and sexually explicit social networking messaging that has instantly changed negatively, the lives of those associated with posting such information.

The tragedy of this phenomenon is that it only takes one mistake to ruin the reputation and lives of all involved. Without ample Internet laws in place and lack of standards, including—moral standards and with the Freedom of the Press which allow us to express our thoughts, ideas, and differences without truly assessing the possible damage and consequences we can cause to ourselves and others, if wisdom is not applied...

We must take a conscious approach of responsibility for the information we send across this marvelous world- wide-web of communications. Our indiscriminate reason to post our beliefs, feelings, passions and desires confirms a growing universal disrespect for God, His principles and humanity.

We cannot de-value the reputation of our leaders, citizens, and our world with the stroke of the keypad and the click of a mouse. Sound judgment, discretion, and wisdom must be applied and practiced before pressing the **Send Button** most likely to destinations unknown. Oftentimes, these communiques are saved forever in the archives of our personal computers and the Cyber-vaults of the Information Cloud.

The negative information that you send out can be used adversely against you for social, criminal or personal evaluation and possible consideration for future opportunities must compel you and I to practice integrity and common sense when social networking.

WARNING:

For example, Fox News reported in March 2012, a few cases that are setting legal precedence with these newly classified criminal offenses. Cyber-crimes are changing the way our judicial systems prosecute individuals committing so-called Internet transgressions.

Sext Messaging: In the Fight Against Teen Sexting, Lawmakers Work to Avoid Turning Kids into Criminals.

Sending out explicit photos from their cell phones can wreck the lives of teens, but experts say lawmakers who seek to tackle the issue often run into unintended consequences of their own. Spurred on by cases of explicit cell phone photos gone viral and bringing dangerous shame and death to their subjects, legislators in 20 states have passed laws making so-called "sext messaging"—sending explicit messages or photos via cell phone—a misdemeanor or even criminal act. But new laws aimed at teen sexting have often criminalized the behavior of naïve teens and even unwitting recipients of the images. Some states have classified teens as sex offenders and even charged them with child pornography, all in a well-intentioned effort to save kids from their own bad behavior. Most recently, New Hampshire joined the effort with a proposed bill that could carry criminal penalties for teens who engage in sexting (Perry Chiaramonte).

Cyber Bullying

The digital world makes communication fast and easy, yet its drawbacks are many: it's highly conducive to impulsive behavior, it's difficult to accurately convey tone and intention, and it's nearly impossible to erase something once it's posted Online. Children need to understand the limitations and dangers of this form of communication, and those missteps Online can have a devastatingly long-term impact in the real world of social media.

The anonymity of the Internet has made it easier for people to be mean to each other, and given rise to a whole new type of bullying: cyber-bullying. A study by isafe.org found that 58 percent of fourth- through eighth-graders have had mean or hurtful things said to them Online, and (even more disturbingly) 53 percent admitted to having said something mean or hurtful to another person Online. Help your children understand the type of behavior that constitutes cyber bullying so they can avoid cyber-bullies and avoid engaging in acts of cyber-bullying.

In addition to monitoring your child's Online behavior, encourage him or her to have a robust social life in the real world – the environment in which we really learn how to behave with others. Social Networking and Media is a wonderful tool for communicating that has revolutionized a generation. However, the many mysteries of its efficiencies' and deficiencies of rules and regulations are still in the infancy stage as our law makers determine how to incorporate electronic crimes into our legal systems for prosecution since there are very few cases to use as precedence.

We must police and govern ourselves responsibly as we move forward in this marvelous world called 'Social Networking, Media and Technology and safely integrate these vast resources of information to its users no matter where it originates or where it terminates. We must also cultivate integral, mutually rewarding relationships in order to bridge the differences between cultures, ages, ethnicities, and generations. We have never had such diversity as we are experiencing in today's global community and economy.

The information age has made our world smaller than ever before. People of all ages are grouped together and co-laboring as well as older workers staying on the job well past their normal age of retirement. Social Networking, Media and Technology has created and interesting paradox:

The young have a chance to teach the older regarding technology and change, and the older have a chance to teach the young; wisdom, principles, understanding, values, and solid work ethics. Social networking, however, has not been a smooth integration and must be addressed on every level in the work place and society.

We are rapidly becoming divided technologically and informationally. We must turn this ensuing gulf into an oasis of opportunity and prosperity for all citizens. The Internet has opened a whole new world of *cyber or virtual* relationships, meaning that your interaction is with some form of technology as the mediator. Social networking threatens the very basic concept of personalized communication.

There are thousands of websites that give the user the feeling of human interaction, but in actuality; they are slowly eroding our society into 'Clandestine Specialist' hiding behind our colorful animated screens as we are less engaging with one another. Many people are becoming cyber addicts by spending hours, sometimes days or even months, on the computer or other devices social networking. Unfortunately, many marriages, families, relationships, and friendships are being and have been destroyed because of these addictions and breeched confidentiality.

We have not acknowledged this problem as clinical yet, but I believe we will start to see the negative effects of social networking in the near future. In many companies, the telephone has become a secondary method of communication. My years in the Telecom Industry allowed me to see this metamorphosis slowly transform and isolate entire departments in some companies, especially in large corporations and governmental agencies; virtually breeding colonies within these entities.

Moreover, with the tightening of security and surveillance being prioritized throughout the world, this mentality further alienates and enhances the chance for paranoia to run rampant in our ever growing private society. We must get back to cultivating face-to-face relationships and friendships. Technology should never replace human relations; instead, it should improve them. Social networking sites can never be a substitute for personal socializing. We must re-institute and encourage engagement of people through community involvement and civic participation in the traditional method of basic friendship and universal relations.

We must all learn about these marvelous technological media tools that have revolutionized a culture and have made life more convenient and people more accessible from afar. The social media, however, has also divided the less technical savvy user and disadvantaged. Regrettably, a sub-culture is also being created involuntarily that will never grasp this fascinating world because of their limited access to technology and their financial disabilities. Our governments must make this technology as affordable and readily available as possible to every citizen.

Only time will be our barometer for where our society is headed with this great divide of the informed and the uninformed. Presently, technology is the driving force behind any great nation and its citizens. Information is revolutionizing people and their countries faster than any industry in the history of our existence. The rapidity of valuable information can be the difference between immediate success and or prolonged failure. Social networking is here to stay, and when governments, businesses, and mainstream society adopt these practices, we must integrate them into our daily lives.

I repeat, "We must integrate them into our daily lives!" The following are a few social networking sites you should visit and connect to: Based on 2015 registered users by each company. Facebook (3.9 Billion users and counting), Instagram (80 Million and counting) Twitter (230 million and counting), Linkedin (277 Million and counting), and YouTube (serving 2 billion videos a day).

In the 2008, presidential election, social networking became the catalyst that propelled then Senator, Barak Obama into being elected the first African American President of the United States of America. Now, as president he is implementing these social networking tools as one of his methods for reaching a cross-culture of citizens.

The USA TODAY news publication posted an article regarding electronic outreach:

President Obama uses his Blackberry to communicate with supporters. Today's forum is his first on Twitter:

President seeks new perspectives during Twitter Forum (July 6, 2011). "The goal is to try and find new opportunities to connect with Americans throughout the country,' said Macon Phillips, director of new media for the White House. "The focus is to bring in a lot of new perspectives" (David Jackson, USA TODAY). The fact that companies are posting employment solicitations for people with social networking experience is an indication of the importance of it in the market place.

www.monster.com lists the following job position as significant to growth for companies:

Social Media Manager

Hiring demand: 1.50 active job seekers for everyopen position

Annual salary range: $38,960-$71,820
10-year growth projection: 24%

Job description: Update your status. Facebook, Twitter, and other "shared" sites aren't just for friends anymore. There're integral-vital components uniquely assembled of specialized, organized with professional, and corporate communications strategies, too. Companies are throwing money at folks who understand how to use social media to build brands and expand markets. Look at Facebook's more than 4 Billion active users, and it's easy to see the potential in this relatively new field. Companies require bachelor's degree in journalism, marketing or communication is preferred.

Our society has changed forever. We will be inundated with information flowing strategically and perpetually from spheres of positive as well as negative origins. Our responsibility is to decipher through these mountains of data streaming endlessly to distract, attack, retract, or impact your life. It's imperative that we all learn to engage ourselves using these ever-changing, advancing social networking and media connecting tools.

However, we can never allow them to alienate us nor evolve our society into a cyber-world of impersonal, useless, redundant message-swappers (with most not being of any true importance). Nothing will ever take the place of the human touch, no matter how many colors the screen has or how fast it can surf to the other side of the world.

Facebook

Twitter

Linkedin

Instagram

faither.com

SUMMARY

In summary, the following are a group of affirming faith-facts. Along your journey this list will prove helpful when a little voice speaks to you whose mission is to devalue your faith-filled walk with the Lord. Don't listen!

FAITH FACTS

- **Faith** to one man may mean something microscopic; to another, it could mean enormously gigantic. It's up to you!

- **Faith** has no boundaries; it is contained only in the mind of the believer.

- **Faith** is by far the most intriguing *gift* God has allowed us to control after love itself.

- **Faith** is NOT age appropriate. It works forever...

- **Faith** can be activated regardless of where you are economically, socially, academically, medically, physically and spiritually.

- **Faith** defies sickness and even death.

- **Faith** positions itself in the "NOW" and waits for further command and action...

- **Faith** says, "I can!"

- **Faith** says, "I cannot stop!"

- **Faith** says, "I will not let you stop!"

- Faith says, "I will!"

- Faith says, "I must!"

- Faith says, "I know!"

- Faith says, "I see!"

- Faith says, "I have!"

- Faith says, "I believe.... "

- Faith says, "Let's do it!"

- Faith says, "Let's do it NOW!"

- Faith requires corresponding **action** and **movement** towards the target from the believer to fully endure to the end.

- Faith never fails, but failing to use Faith always does!

- Faith says, "Thank You Jesus!"

Finally, I leave with you the words in which we begin this study: **"Now faith is the substance of things hoped for, the evidence of things not seen"** (Hebrew 11:1)

You Must Be Willing to...

- Commit to a life of prayer and without distraction

- Make God's ways your way

- Minister to Him in prayer as He reveals His plan

- Serve others as you await full manifestation of your vision

- Seek the baptism in the Holy Ghost

- Identify that ministry of expertise which belongs to you

- Prepare to operate in a spirit of excellence

Love and believe God no matter how things look, in spite of opposition Then you too will abide peacefully, in full provision and with great potential. God will overwhelm you with His ability and willingness to shower you with favor, grace, substance and more importantly: LOVE NEVER FAILS— don't you dare quit! EVER!!

Now... Faith Is...,
Fray White

Index and References

Serving:
http://www.brainyquote.com/quotes/quotes/m/mahatmag
an150725. ml Mahatma Gandhi Page 22

President Clinton's Quote:
http://www.finance.yahoo.com/blogs/daily-ticker/
president-bill-clinton-yes-american-dream-under-assault-
231659873.html (Aaron Task | Daily Ticker). Page 56

Mitt Romney's Quote:
http://www.boston.com/news/politics/articles/2011/10/07/
romneygodwantsustoleadnotfollow/ Page 58

Myles Munroe, Passing It On Pages Hachette Book Group
(2011). www.faithwords.com Page 65

A 2008 goal setting study sponsored by the Ford
Foundation found the following interesting statistics:
http://ezinearticles.com/?The-Top-3%25-Who-Achieve-
Their-Goals-Have-a-Secret&id=2865364 Page 82

Writing a Business plan:
http://www.inc.com/guides/201107/how-to-write-an-
operational-plan-for-your-small-business.html
Inc Magazine (Darren Dahl). Page 83

Steve Jobshttp://www.goodreads.com/quotes/772887-the-
only-way-to-do-great-work-is-to-love Page 102
Mr. Edison
quotes,http://www.brainyquote.com/quotes/authors/t/tho
masaedison.html Page 103

Mission Statement: Chick-Fil-A Page 134

Chick-Fil-A- (Josh Cody, 2007-05). Page 134
http://www.churchmarketingsucks.com/2007/05 chick-
fil- a-church-marketing/

Hobby Lobby: Missions Statement Page 135

Tina Turner: "What's Love Got to With It" Page 168
Album, Private Dancer (1984) Page 168

Mahatma Gandhi
http://www.beliefnet.com/Quotes/Relationships/M/Mahat
ma-Gandhi/Love-never-claims.aspx Page 170

Director, Robert Townsend, filmed a scene in the movie,
"The Five Heart Beats."(Movie 1991) Page 173

"Fountains of Pleasure" Al-Sayed Haroun Ibn Hussein Al-
Makhzoumi (1986) Page 186

Myles Munroe, Passing It On Pages Hachette Book Group
(2011). www.faithwords.com Page 236 and 239

The Gettysburg Address
www.abrahamlincolnonline.org/lincoln/speeches/gettysb
urg.htm Page 194

President Kennedy's Inaugural Speech
www.jfklibrary.org/Asset-
Viewer/BqXIEM9F4024ntFl7SVAjA.aspx Page 196

Social Networking Media, Wikipedia, Page 214

Sexting:http://www.foxnews.com/politics/2012/03/05/in-
effort-to-curb-teen-sexting-state-lawmakers-work-to-
avoid-turning-kids-into/#ixzzlwlGctZi8(By Perry
Chiaramonte / March 05, 2012). Page 215

President Obama, Black
Berry,http://www.usatoday30.usatoday.com/news/washin
gton/2011-07-05-obama-twitter-town-hall_n.htmUSA
Today, (David Jackson, 2011) Page 219

Social Media Manager: http://www.jobs.monster.com/v-
marketing-q-social-media-director-jobs. Aspx Page 220

About The Author

Fray White, is a humble father of three beautiful young adults, a licensed Minister of the Gospel of Jesus Christ.

Fray enlisted into the US Armed Forces where he served in the Berlin Brigade, Berlin Germany. He was assigned to the Berlin Consultant—performing duties as a Telephone Installer and Communication Specialist.

After honorably discharging, Fray founded Meridian Consulting Group Inc. (www.1meridian.com.) A company providing Telecom and IT Consulting, Training, Voice, Data, Video, Wireless and Security services to several thousand private corporations, governmental agencies, institutions of higher learning and many other sectors of business around the country.

Fray has employed, trained and inspired 100's employees with some creating new companies that compete, provide employment and make considerable contributions to our local economies. His insight and vision enables him to see beyond the present, interact successfully with a multiplicity of people, cultures as well as nationalities; giving him a broader prospective on world views and international events.

He has traveled extensively abroad: Italy, Germany, Austria, The Netherlands, Portugal, The Caribbean, and Mexico—often residing amongst the locals in fellowship and in harmony. Fray has a unique ability to cultivate the gifts lying dormant within individuals, inspiring them to move to greater heights.

An avid golfer and sports enthusiast he has played on several National Championship Fast-Pitch Softball Teams and is a member of the National Softball Hall of Fame and Museum in Oklahoma City, Oklahoma.

His love for Jesus Christ and people compelled him to seek a deeper relationship with Him in April 2004. He made a commitment to fully serve Him the remainder of his life. Fray has a heart for mentoring youth and men, has launched his foundation (www.boysandmentoring.org) in 2015. He began his ministerial career as a college professor at Life Christian University in 2010, teaching accredited Leadership, Theology and Spiritual Growth courses.

Fray also facilitated Men's Ministry Groups in leadership. He has begun a new life in the Ministry, Publishing, Multi-Media and Christian Entertainment Business and by the will of God hope to build a legacy that shall remain from generation to generation.